Gratitude Healing

By

Monte J. Meldman M.D.

ISBN: 0-75963-956-6

This book is printed on acid free paper.

1stBooks-rev. 07/10/01

Do good, be good and you'll have good.

Grandma Sarah Clara Bortin

A person can almost be defined by his or her attitude toward gratitude

Elie Wiesel

Gratitude is not only the greatest of all the virtues,
but the parent of all the others

Cicero (106-43 B.C.)

Table of Contents

MONTE'S GRATITUDE

To Aunt Belle Ruppa for medical school with Father Berendt

To my father for love and fishing; to my Mother for love and food and swimming lessons and music lessons and fright.

James Shutkin, Bobby Rice, Bobby Perles, Art Gronik, Doug Mann, Dan Albert, Syd Altman, Dick Urdan, Bob Hyman, Morris Squire, Bernie Newman, Elton Mendeloff, Ernie Wolf, Stan Kaplan, Adolph Stern, Rex Ruppa, Morty Bortin for friendship.

Mr. Chapitis, Mr. Brewer, Ms. Maloney, Mr. Ingrelli, Miss Moss, Miss Cashman, Bergen Evans, Clem Fox, Walter Zeit for teaching.

AMERICA. Gloria for love and affection.

For being a doctor and feeling that is my calling in life.

For Karen, Diana, Barbara, Larry, Lauren, Noel, Oren, Ariella, Elan, Jay, Jeffrey, Leah

For June, June, Jane, June, Jean, Barbara, Jean, Jacob, Joanne

For Dr. Duncan, Dr. Shulman, Burton, Clifford

For Valium, Oh Lord, For Valium.

For flowers, trees, sunshine, nature, lakes, oceans, fishing, and just knowing it is all there.

For the houses, food, clothes, parties, and fun times and the fear and negative thinking and doubt and all the failures, depressions and worries.

For my offices, computer and piano and Korg Triton and Steinway that Gloria gave me.

For my patients. I love you the max.

For my shame and inability to stand a compliment and shyness and the bad self image that never changes.

For Being A Doctor.

For the beautiful music.

For all the toys I play with.

For relentless enthusiasm and lack of follow through, for being lazy.

For Eldee Young, Michael Arnapole, and Curtis Robinson.

For my many bad qualities.

For Morton Arboretum with Gloria, and Canadian fishing with Eddy, Cliffy, George, and Larry.

Introduction

I rediscovered gratitude during my treatment with Dr. Bernard Shulman. The rediscovery happened after a long period of the ingrate state expressed in my treatment as complaining, moaning and worrying about events that were not. This realization came to me when I was wondering about all of my lamenting and self-pity and anxiety, when my life was going pretty well. I suddenly realized that I was moaning about nothing real, that I was complaining about things that did not exist, and that I was trying to adapt to events that weren't.

I have long been preoccupied with loss. I guess I wanted to become a doctor to help other people as a defense against feelings of loss, so it isn't all bad. I always worry about losing what I have, and sometimes worry about losing what I don't have! Sick, Sick, Sick. The more you have, the more you have to lose, so the more anxiety you have for fear of losing it. Dr. Shulman let me moan, complain and go on with my consummate negativity, occasionally responding with some humor from time to time. I rediscovered gratitude trying to get out of the pile of negativity that has always swamped my life. It came back to me as totally obvious, for I have spent many years taking care of alcoholics and drug addicts (some 15,00 or more) and "The attitude of gratitude" is the central theme in AA, EA, CA, OA, and Alanon. I have discussed gratitude in depth with 15,000 people and was real good at teaching others to feel gratitude and get into that mode of living in the 12 step recovery program. I guess the more you talk about it, the more you keep it on your lips and it doesn't get integrated with your feelings, thoughts and actions. So I wore gratitude on my sleeve and in my mouth and that kept it from getting it integrated inside. So this book is an attempt to get it inside of me and to help you get it inside of you so you can really get The Attitude of Gratitude and all that it can do to improve your life.

I express my gratitude to Dr. Shulman and my wonderful wife, Gloria. I thank Aunt Belle Ruppa, Uncle John Ruppa, my wonderful mother, Rose and my terrific father, Edward H. for all the gifts they gave me. I thank my teachers, my tutor, and the authors of all the books I have read; the EA program for helping me get some sanity. I thank all my enemies and my partners in psychiatry, the staffs at Forest Hospital and Westlake Community Hospital for all they did to and for me. I appreciate all the people I have let down and all those who let me down. I give thanks to all the people I envy and who are superior to me. Most of all, I appreciate the sun, trees, eyes, ears and the music. Negative thinking has made my life very difficult. I am now a grateful negative thinker, not much improvement, but some change and some place to go to feel better. I appreciate that. And you too. Love you, Monte

Belle Bortin Ruppa
1920
(1898-1981)

Belle Bortin Ruppa overcame a difficult, poverty-defined childhood. After her father abandoned the family, her brother Herman, three years Belle's senior, left school at the age of 13 to help support the family. Their mother also worked outside the home to help make ends meet. There were five children, and as the eldest daughter, Belle took on many parental responsibilities as a pre-teen. All the Bortin children graduated college and graduate school.

Belle Bortin graduated from North Division High School in Milwaukee and entered Marquette University in 1917. With considerable fanfare from the press, Belle passed her Wisconsin bar exam in 1920. Not only was she one of the few women to enter the legal profession that year, at the age of 22 she was the youngest woman ever to pass the bar in Wisconsin.

Upon graduation from Marquette, she was quoted in a local newspaper as saying, "My ambition if to become the head of a legal aid society for women...My admittance to the bar is due to perseverance and being able to accomplish what I set out to do."

She started out in private practice as a criminal defense lawyer. In 1920, after Women's Suffrage in the State of Wisconsin, Belle became the first woman to run for an elected office in Wisconsin. Running on the Republican ticket, she made an unsuccessful bid to represent the Sixth District as a state senator.

In 1927, as "the Chairman of the National Women's Party and attorney handling Wisconsin's new fight for equal rights," Belle published an article about women's rights in Wisconsin. In 1930 she was the "state chairman of the Equal Rights International, a feminist organization seeking 'equality for women.'"

In 1921 Belle married attorney John Ruppa. After the birth of her son, Rex, in 1922, she took a year off from her law career. In 1923 Belle Bortin Ruppa returned to the courtroom, practicing law with her husband until they both retired in 1950. They also owned six hotels, among many other properties. She died in 1981.

http://www.wisbar.org/pioneers/bios/ruppa.html

What is Gratitude?

Gratitude as a feeling begins with receiving a gift, or construing an event in life as a gift. Then the person feels gratitude to the giver for the gift, say thanks and feels appreciation for the gift. Then the person shows gratitude by "putting something back in" in return for what has been received. It is not enough just to say thanks and feel grateful. The requirement for true gratitude is to spread gratitude around to all the people in your life. From this experience it is possible to look for gratitude opportunities, moments of gratitude and to create gratitude in yourself and others by being a model of gratitude. That is the way to discharge the obligation you feel for receiving the gift in the first place. Thus Gratitude becomes a state of mind, a place in which you can find inner peace and a sense of wholeness in your life. Gratitude integrates all the conflicted and broken parts of your life into a meaningful whole and the process of doing that is what we call Gratitude Healing.

Gratitude—Noun, gratitude, thankfulness, feeling of obligation, sense of obligation, acknowledgment, recognition, thanksgiving, thanksgiving, giving thanks: thankful good will. Thanks, praise, benediction: paean; grace before meals, grace after meals; thanks offering.

Verb—Be grateful. Adj.: thank; give thanks, render thanks, return thanks, offer thanks, tender thanks, to acknowledge a gift, feel under an obligation, be under an obligation, not look a gift horse in the mouth; never forget, overflow with gratitude, thank one's lucky stars; My cup runneth over.

Adj.—Grateful, thankful, obliged, beholden, indebted to, under obligation. Thank Heaven!

Gratitude is a central concept in many religions, where gratitude to God for gifts given is a core idea. This is revealed in Buddhism, Judaism, and Christianity. In Judaism, the Ten Commandments are the gift from God, and a Jewish life is devoted to fulfilling *mitzvot*, or performing all of the commandments given by God in the Torah. In a similar way, Jesus is God's gift to the people of the world and gratitude is expressed by accepting Jesus (believing in Him) and showing His way to man. The reward for this is eternal life.

Antonym—The opposite of gratitude is taking life for granted, taking people for granted, and taking your eyes and sight for granted. Beyond that, the ingrate state is characterized by intense egoism in which the "great I am" feels self-sufficient, and does not appreciate what others have done nor what he owes to others and America. The ingrate state does not pay back for what he/she has been given.

GRATITUDE

Gratitude unlocks the fullness of life. It turns what we have into enough, and more. It turns denial into acceptance, chaos to order, confusion to clarity. It can turn a meal into a feast, a house into a home, a stranger into a friend. Gratitude makes sense of our past, brings peace for today, and creates a vision for tomorrow.

~ Melody Beattie ~

A proud man is seldom a grateful man, for he never thinks he gets as much as he deserves.

~ Henry Ward Beecher ~

Unto every one that hath shall be given, and he shall have abundance but from him that hath not shall be taken away even that which he hath. (Matthew)

~ Bible ~

There is a calmness to a life lived in Gratitude, a quiet joy.

~ Ralph H. Blum ~

Because gratification of a desire leads to the temporary stilling of the mind and the experience of the peaceful, joyful Self it's no wonder that we get hooked on thinking that happiness comes from the satisfaction of desires. This is the meaning of the old adage, "Joy is not in things, it is in us."

~ Joan Borysenko ~

Both abundance and lack exist simultaneously in our lives, as parallel realities. It is always our conscious choice which secret garden we will tend...when we choose not to focus on what is missing from our lives but are grateful for the abundance that's present—love, health, family friends, work, the joys of nature and personal pursuits that bring us pleasure—the wasteland of illusion falls away and we experience Heaven on earth.

~ Sarah Ban Breathnach ~

I don't like it when people on the street say "smile" or "cheer up." It's a real cheap line. I'm feeling good. I'm feeling real grateful for everything. It's a solid time in my life. When people say I look sad, they're wrong.

~ Nicholas Cage ~

Remember that not to be happy is not to be grateful.

~ Elizabeth Carter ~

Feeling grateful or appreciative of someone or something in your life actually attracts more of the things that you appreciate and value into your life.

~ Northrup Christiane ~

Most people return small favors, acknowledge medium ones and repay greater ones—with ingratitude.

~ Benjamin Franklin ~

To speak gratitude is courteous and pleasant, to enact gratitude is generous and noble, but to live gratitude is to touch Heaven.

~ Johannes A. Gaertner ~

He that has satisfied his thirst turns his back on the well.

~ Baltasar Gracian ~

True thanksgiving means that we need to thank God for what He has done for us, and not to tell Him what we have done for Him.

~ George R. Hendrick ~

For today and its blessings, I owe the world an attitude of gratitude.

~ Clarence E. Hodges ~

We seldom find people ungrateful so long as it is thought we can serve them.

~ Francois De La Rochefoucauld ~

Do you realize what this means? The fact of being alive...I still find it staggering that I am here at all.

~ Christopher Leach ~

One can never pay in gratitude, one can only pay "in kind" somewhere else in life.

~ Anne Morrow Lindbergh ~

Nothing purchased can come close to the renewed sense of gratitude for having family and friends.

~ Courtland Milloy ~

Gratitude is the heart's memory.

~ French Proverb ~

Two kinds of gratitude: The sudden kind we feel for what we take; the larger kind we feel for what we give.

~ Edwin Arlington Robinson ~

It is another's fault if he be ungrateful, but it is mine if I do not give. To find one thankful man, I will oblige a great many that are not so.

~ Seneca ~

Gratitude is a sickness suffered by dogs.

~ Joseph Stalin ~

Gratitude is our most direct line to God and the angels. If we take the time, no matter how crazy and troubled we feel, we can find something to be thankful for. The more we seek gratitude, the more reasons the angels will give us for gratitude and joy to exist in our lives.

~ <u>Terry Lynn Taylor</u> ~

God has two dwellings; one in heaven, and the other in a meek and thankful heart.

~ <u>Izaak Walton</u> ~

Gratitude is not only the memory but the homage of the heart rendered to God for His goodness.

~ <u>Nathaniel P. Willis</u> ~

Being a Jew is synonymous with expressing gratitude. Our matriarch Leah taught us to see everything in life as a gift.

By Lori Palatnik

> *"From the day that God created the world, there was no one who thanked God until Leah came and thanked Him."*
> (The Talmud)

Leah, married to Jacob, was one of the mothers of the Jewish people. In the passage above, the Talmud is referring to the birth of Leah's fourth son, Judah. The name Judah shares the same root in Hebrew as the word *todah*, meaning "thank you." But what does the Talmud mean when it says that Leah was the first person to ever really thank God?

Abraham never thanked God? Noah never thanked God? Sarah never thanked God? Of course, they did. In fact, many people had thanked God in the Torah long before Leah. Therefore, the Talmud must be telling us that there was something special about Leah's thankfulness. Her gratitude must have been somehow truer and deeper than that of anyone who had come before her.

By understanding what made Leah's gratitude special, we will learn what true gratefulness is all about.

SEEING EVERYTHING AS A GIFT

Leah was a prophetess who knew that the Jewish nation was destined to descend from the 12 sons of Jacob, her husband. Each tribe would be a foundation stone that would shape our history. Jacob's sons would come from four women: Leah, Rachel, Bilha and Zilpah. Leah expected that each woman would have 3 sons.

Leah's thankfulness for the birth of Judah was deeper and more heartfelt because he was unexpected.

Judah was Leah's fourth son. She recognized that he was one more than her share. Her thankfulness for Judah was deeper and more heartfelt because he was unexpected. He was a gift.

This is how we are supposed to view *everything* in life. Every ray of sunshine, every child, every breath—they are all gifts from God.

The mistake of thinking anything is owed to us blocks us from gratitude.

People sometimes don't appreciate sight until they meet someone who is blind. We shouldn't wait until we are sick to appreciate our health. We should count our blessings every day and take pleasure in the miraculous gifts bestowed upon us

Beginning The Day With Gratitude

Jewish consciousness says that every morning we should rise with the prayer, *Modeh Ani.* I am grateful to God for bringing life to me each and every day."

At our time of sorrow, when we have lost a loved one, we are forced to stand and face our own mortality. We do not live forever, and we do not know from one day to the next when our time will come. All we can do is say, *Modeh Ani.* "I am grateful to God, for giving me another day, and another opportunity to use it wisely."

Our religion is called "Judaism" from Judah. The essence of being a Jew is to be thankful. Realize, as Leah did, that every moment of life is a gift. Open the gift and take pleasure in its Source.

Adapted from Lori Palatnik's <u>Remember My Soul!</u> Buy the book from <u>amazon.com</u>

An Anonymous Jewish Gratitude Blessing

I believe that any person who has wandered into the "settlement of the Twelve Steps from the wilderness of active addiction qualifies to say this blessing on all four counts.

In the Shulchan Aruch, Orach Chaim (219:1-3), we learn:

Four categories of people should express particular gratitude to God:

Those who have completed sea voyages, those who have arrived at settlements after passing through the desert, those who have recovered from an illness, and those who have been freed from prison.

What is the blessing they recite?

Blessed are You, Lord our god,
Ruler of the universe,
Who is gracious even to those who may not be worthy—
You have graciously extended great kindness to me.

Those who hear the recitation of this blessing should respond:

May the One Who has graciously extended great kindness to you continue to do so

(translation from Where Heaven and Earth Touch, by Danny Siegel c 1989, Jason Aronson)

Our "voyage," wherever it took us, was one long, strange trip. We have seen the monsters of the deep, and it was us. We have suffered the self-inflicted isolation of those who have to endure long trips at sea. And we have been a bit warped by a kind of emotional scurvy, to the point where expressing our feelings and relating to and trusting others are fraught with all the fear and wonderment of a baby's tottering first steps. Many of us have never lived life on its own terms, but we are here to learn...

And we have been through the wilderness too—whether reduced to "on the street" living or not, our lives themselves became parched with hopelessness and dusty with lies. And it doesn't matter whether our journey was for forty months or forty years—if our journey has brought us to the spiritual reawakening and life-renewing miracle of recovery, then we have come to the right place.

Recovered from illness? No...not yet, but recovering. As one of my best NA buddies, Paul B. put it, "If they ever find a pill to cure addiction, I'll take two of them!"

But "freed from prison?" Definitely! I have spoken on behalf of my fellowship once at a prison, and with God's help, I will do so again. I will tell you the three "revelations" that experience gave me.

Number one, that it was only because recovery caught me before the police did, that enabled me to be sitting on the other side of the room that night—looking back, there were more than a few close encounters with the law and incriminating circumstances that could easily have led to a different sort of "time."

Number two, I found that I had at least as much in common with my brother addicts in prison as I do with my fellow congregants at a Shabbat morning *kiddush*—maybe even more, as we recovering addicts are no longer so socially inclined to leave out the bad stuff. One of the more significant spiritual lessons I have learned in my recovery is to look beyond appearances and to realize that, especially in matters of the heart and soul, most people have more in common than the history of human intolerance would ever suggest.

But the most exhilarating discovery of all was how great it feels to walk out of a prison and not be stopped! Joni Mitchell's wise observation—that you never know what you've got until it's gone (or until you're this close to losing it)—remains as true as ever. Indeed, that recollection of being on the precipice of losing it all is a powerful motivator of many an addict's recovery—and continuing gratitude.

And what does it mean to be freed from prison? To feel a giddy bit more alive and vibrant. To be willing and able to take some time to stop and smell the roses, watch the sun set, or head over to a meeting. And most of all—to have choices, choices that always seemed to dance between our ears but never beyond when we were still using.

I remember a line from a Bob Dylan song back in the early seventies: "Sometimes I think this world is one big prison yard, and some of us are prisoners; the rest of us are guards." And that's what I believe today—that we're either prisoners of our own passions, past, and/or distorted thinking—or else we grow to the point where we incorporate some spiritual principles into our lives. And then guard them. When we care enough about something, we want to keep and protect it. The Hebrew term for someone who observes the Sabbath, for example, is *shomer Shabbes*—literally, a Sabbath guarder or guardian.

So maybe Mr. Dylan was right, and maybe that is the great spiritual challenge that ultimately confronts us all: to grow beyond the confines of our own ego, selfishness, impulses and arrogance by adopting spiritually healthier principles and practices in our lives that uphold us even as we try to uphold them. We may have learned this lesson the hard way, but maybe that will make it harder to forget. It certainly is one more thing to be grateful for—and also well deserving of the Jewish gratitude blessing. It is, I suspect, the only blessing that can never be recited in vain.

Aaron Z.

Gratitude

For those who care to know

The deep core of America's blessed greatness'

The imperfect skin of a God-given fruit

Never reflects its innermost sweetness...

Linh Duy Vo

No duty is more urgent than that of returning thanks.

Unknown

"Thank God—every morning when you get up—that you have something to do which must be done, whether you like it or not. Being forced to work, and forced to do your best, will breed in you a hundred virtues which the idle never know."

Charles Kingsley

Let us be grateful to people who make us happy; they are the charming gardeners who make our souls blossom."

Marcel Proust

"What sunshine is to flowers, smiles are to humanity. These are but trifles, to be sure; but, scattered along life's pathway, the good they do is inconceivable."

Joseph Addison

"Gratitude unlocks the fullness of life. It turns what we have into enough, and more. It turns denial into acceptance, chaos to order, confusion to clarity. It can turn a meal into a feast, a house into a home, a stranger into a friend. Gratitude makes sense of our past, brings peace for today, and creates a vision for tomorrow."

Melody Beattie

"The sun was shining in my eyes, and I could barely see
To do the necessary task that was allotted me.
Resentment of the vivid glow, I started to complain—
When all at once upon the air I heard the blindman's cane."

Earl Musselman

"As we express our gratitude, we must never forget that the highest appreciation is not to utter words, but to live by them."

John Fitzgerald Kennedy

"A contented mind is the greatest blessing a man can enjoy is this world."

Joseph Addison

"To educate yourself for the feeling of gratitude means to take nothing for granted, but to always seek out and value the kind that will stand behind the action. Nothing that is done for you is a matter of course. Everything originates in a will for the good, which is directed at you. Train yourself never to put off the word or action for the expression of gratitude."

Albert Schweitzer

"Most of us, swimming against the tides of trouble the world knows nothing about, need only a bit of praise or encouragement—and we will make the goal."

Jerome P. Fleishman

"Gratitude is not only the greatest of virtues, but the parent of all the others."

Cicero (140 B.C.)

"Nothing is more honorable than a grateful heart."

Seneca

"True thanksgiving means that we need to thank God for what He has done for us, and not to tell Him what we have done for Him."

George R. Hendrick

"Gratitude is the fairest blossom which springs from the soul."

Henry Ward Beecher

"Thankfulness is the beginning of gratitude.
Gratitude is the completion of thankfulness.
Thankfulness may consist merely of words.
Gratitude is shown in acts."

David O. McKay

BE THANKFUL

Be thankful that you don't already have everything you desire,
if you did, what would there be to look forward to?
Be thankful when you don't know something
for it gives you the opportunity to learn.

Be thankful for the difficult times.
during those times you grow.
Be thankful for your limitations
because they give you opportunities for improvement.

Be thankful for each new challenge
because it will build your strength and character.
Be thankful for your mistakes
They will teach you valuable lessons.

Be thankful when you're tired and weary
because it means you've made a difference.
It is easy to be thankful for the good things.
a life of rich fulfillment comes to those who are also thankful for the setbacks.

Author Unknown

Yo buddy, nobody owes you anything. You do not deserve anything for what you have done, or for what you have suffered. You are not entitled to anything. The mistake of thinking any thing is owed to us, like blaming, blocks us from gratitude. Get into Gratitude and say "Thank you for what I have been given" Thank you for my obesity, my diet, my feeling of deprivation and frustration and anger and the injustice I feel that it is so hard to lose weight. Thank you for hunger. It means I am losing weight.

THOUGHTS ON GRATITUDE

By Masai Jones

Meditation

Some people meditate for an hour. I have been meditating on Gratitude for the last three months. Some meditations are private, internalized reflections, my meditation of Gratitude has been very public, with my asking almost anyone who would listen and talk about what their thoughts were on gratitude. And I still don't feel that I have come to the conclusion of my meditation, it's a work in progress. So what I am going to speak on today, "Having an Attitude of Gratitude", is to be understood as a collection of thoughts, prayers, reflections and input from several sources. I have discussed my reflections with a few people here, I have gone to my source materials on Islam, Sufis, Native Cultures, Christianity, Taoism, etc. to glean some wisdom from thinkers more profound than I.

Wonder

I've discovered that one of the avenues to Gratitude is through Wonder, having a sense of wonder about Life. Although I don't think that having wonder is a necessary prerequisite for gratitude, it enhances it, makes it more majestic, allows us to see the world as a miraculous place, a marvelous creation of God's invention.

With wonder we see the world anew almost daily, in each person we meet, in each touch. Wonder gives our heart room for expansion, room to hold all that is marvelous, to see it as marvelous. To find the extraordinary in what looks like the ordinary. Wonder helps us to recognize Spirit in its earthly physical manifestation.

Gratitude

I live in a beautiful place with soulful, spiritual people. The natural wonders of light, lake, energy, friendship have filled my expanded heart with gratitude. I have a beautiful home, a wonderful counseling practice, a deeply satisfying position as the Hospice Chaplain. And I never take these things for granted. Gratitude is not taking your life for granted, it's living in the heart with wonder and thankfulness.

This aspect of gratitude is easy to accept and to understand. When life is good we are thankful—although most of us don't give thanks. The next step on my meditation was more difficult to comprehend. The opening occurred while listening to someone expressing her gratitude for her health because her cousin had polio. She said, "there but for God, go I." I understood what she meant by this statement, we all have heard it many times in our culture. But because of my meditation of Gratitude, this time I had to pause and reflect on the inherent meaning of this statement.

If I believe "there but for God go I", then I am seeing my self as separate and luckier than others. I am putting myself above others. I am expressing my gratitude at the expense of another of God's children. And while it is true that we all are different, have more or less money, more or less physical ability, more of less mental prowess, how do we rate ourselves more in God's favor because we have these material and physical attributes? Does God love these others any less? Does having more money or access to resources mean that God blesses us more. How did we begin to equate 'more' with God's blessings in our culture?

I thought about others who have a physical disability. Is it possible that they could be full of gratitude for God's blessing? What about people who live in developing countries without our rich resources? Isn't it possible that they could feel God's grace as well?

It was only yesterday that I found that the expression, "there but for God go I" has been modified from the original quote from Paul in 1 Corinthians 15:10, "But by the grace of God, I am what I am"!!!! What an important revelation! It means something altogether different. "By the Grace of God I am what I am" implies an acceptance of God's grace and hard gifts. This led me to the meditation of acceptance as gratitude.

Acceptance

When life is easy it is easy to feel gratitude. When life gets tougher, what does gratitude look like?

I remembered nine years ago when I got very sick with Lymes Disease; my world was falling apart. I was exhausted all the time, had severe headaches, nerve loss, joint pain. I was unable to continue to work full time. My husband and I had only been married for one year and he was now taking care of me and resenting it. Our marriage was severely strained to the breaking point. On top of that, the same year my father died, we were living in the Bay Area which suffered its worst quake since 1907 and our house was damaged. Outside of our family the world was in chaos too; the Tieneman square massacre, the fall of the Berlin wall and the end to communism as it had been previously. These were turbulent times. This was truly a watershed year.

Yet it was this trial by fire that change my life for the better. I call it my Shamanic initiation. This was the year of my tremendous growth of spirit, of character, of action. This was the year that I grounded in Spirit. I learned the hard lessons and got the hard blessings. I came of age. I grew to become grateful for the illness. It was my opening into higher consciousness.

With all the pain, fatigue and hardship how could I be grateful? How can someone who has been diagnosed with cancer consider himself grateful. How do people who lose their homes to fire consider themselves grateful? What about losing a loved one? How can one affect an Attitude of Gratitude when seeming tragedy befalls us?

I owe this next level of understanding to a dear hospice client who let me interview him for my doctoral thesis. He called me recently to discuss his ideas of gratitude as he nears his death. He wanted to have a witness to all the wonders of his life and the gratitude he feels to God. I asked him to explain how he has gratitude for his illness, the cancer which is taking his life.

He recalled the Old Testament story of Jacob who fought with the angel. He, himself, was like Jacob who wrestled with the stranger (who unbeknownst to him was an Angel). Jacob wouldn't let go until the stranger blessed him and they fought all night. Jacob said, "Give me your blessings and I will let you go! Bless me!" Finally in the morning, both exhausted, Jacob received his blessing from the stranger who then revealed himself to be a messenger of God. My Hospice client said that in a similar way he first struggled with his illness. He struggled for many months and wouldn't let go of the struggle with his illness until he got its blessing! He tried to understand "what is the blessing from this illness? What can I get from this?" And finally, like the stranger/angel blessing Jacob, this man was blessed by the understanding of the illness. And with deep gratitude he realized that through this gift, the gift of the cancer, he has been transformed in his life. It has transformed his relationship with his family and loved ones. It has transformed his relationship with himself. He now recognizes the incredible gift that is his life. This knowing would never have occurred unless for his illness, the blessing, the gift of the illness. He feels so fortunate to have had this experience before he dies. He exemplifies "By the grace of God, I am what I am." This is acceptance of God's plans. This is gratitude through acceptance.

There is also Gratitude as Surrender. When we surrender to Spirit's plan, no matter how seemingly difficult and confusing it seems at the time, we are showing gratitude to the divine. We are moving our egos aside and allowing Spirit to enter. The Tao Te Ching says, "Because he has let go of himself—he is perfectly fulfilled." It also says, "She is like a turtle—wherever she is, she is home." When we are full of acceptance of God's plan, when we surrender to our faith, experiencing the wonder of God's creation, when we have faith that wherever we are is the perfect place for us, despite all the illusions to the contrary, when we carry faith like our home on our back, we have clarity.

Many years ago, my guardian angel gave me this deep knowing. "Clarity is joyousness and joyousness is love." To rise to love is to open our heart. With Wonder, Acceptance, Faith, Surrender, and Love, we show Spirit out of gratitude for all its creation.

In closing I offer a Prayer of Gratitude in the Buddhist Tradition

> We rejoice in all life
>
> We live in all things
> All things live in us
>
> We live by the sun
> We move with the stars
>
> We eat from the earth
> We drink from the rain
>
> We breathe from the air
>
> We share with the creatures
> We have strength through their gifts
>
> We depend on the forests
> We have knowledge through their secrets
>
> We have the privilege of seeing and understanding
> We have the responsibility of caring
> We have the joy of celebrating

Monte J. Meldman M.D.

We are full of the grace of creation
We are graceful
We are grateful
We rejoice in life

On Gratitude And Virtue

A sense of gratitude and indebtedness to others is an important wellspring of a generous and virtuous life. All people can recognize that they are indebted to their parents, who gave them birth and raised them at considerable sacrifice. But our indebtedness extends much further than that. Fundamentally, we are indebted to God our Creator and the powers of nature that nourish and through many hands—that cultivate, harvest, clean, package, transport, sell, and prepare it—we should recognize that we rely on the labors of many people in order to survive. A sense of gratitude to others is thus acknowledging our interdependent existence; it is an antidote to the illusion of egoism. Such gratitude is recalled and expressed in the prayer of grace or thanks offered before meals.

Another dimension of gratitude is directed towards those who are responsible for our education and enlightenment in the way of truth and salvation. Gratitude towards one's teachers, and especially towards the sages and founders of religions who offered their lives to find the truth, is a proper attitude of faith. Most of all, we should be grateful to God, who quietly has been guiding and nurturing each person toward salvation, and without whose grace the world would be plunged in darkness.

And whatever you do, in word or deed, do everything in the name of the Lord Jesus, giving thanks to God the Father through Him. Christianity. Colossians 3.17

O you who believe! Eat of the good things that we have provided for you, and be grateful to God, if it is Him that you worship. Islam. Qur'an 2.172 Colossians 3.17: Cf Psalm 100, p. 202.

God created foods to be received with thanksgiving by those who believe and know the truth. For everything created by God is good, and nothing is to be rejected if it is received with thanksgiving; for then it is consecrated by the word of God and prayer. Christianity 1 Timothy 4.3-5

Abraham caused God's name to be mentioned by all the travelers whom he entertained. For after they had eaten and drunk, and when they arose to bless Abraham, He said to them, "Is it of mine that you have eaten? Surely it is of what belongs to God that you have eaten. So praise and bless Him by whose word the world was created." Judaism. Talmud, Sota 10b

The unworthy man is ungrateful, forgetful of benefits (done to him). This ingratitude, this forgetfulness is congenial to mean people. But the worthy person is grateful and mindful of benefits done to him. This gratitude, this mindfulness, is congenial to the best people. Buddhism. Anguttara Nikaya i.61

One upon whom we bestow kindness but will not express gratitude, is worse than a robber Who carries away our belongings. African Tradional Religions. Yoruba Proverb (Nigeria)

Be not like those who honor their gods in prosperity and curse them in adversity. In pleasure or pain, give thanks! Judaism. Midrash, Mekilta to Exodus 20.20

Even if you cry your heart out, hurt your eyes by constant weeping and even if you lead the life of an ascetic till the end of the world, all these untiring efforts of yours will not be able to make compensation for a tithe of His good will and kindness, for His bounties and munificence and for His mercy and charity in directing you towards the path of truth and religion. Islam (Shiite). Nahjul Balagha, Khutba 57

It is God who has made the night for you, that you may rest therein, and the day, as that which helps you to see. Verily God is full of grace and bounty to men, yet most men give no thanks. It is God who has made for you the earth as a resting place, and the sky as a canopy, and has given you shape—and made your shapes beautiful—and has provided for you sustenance of things pure and good, such is God, your Lord. So glory to God, the Lord of the Worlds! Islam. Qur'an 40.61,64

O my Father, Great Elder, I have no words to thank you, But with your deep wisdom, I am sure that you can see how I value your glorious gifts. O my Father, when I look upon your greatness, I am confounded with awe. O Great Elder, Ruler of all things earthly and heavenly, I am your warrior, Ready to act in accordance with your will. African Traditional Religions. Kikuya Prayer (Kenyan)

You, the World Honored One, are a great benefactor. By doing this rare thing, you taught and benefited us out of your compassion towards us. No one will be able to repay your favors even if he tries to do it For many hundreds of millions of *kalpas*. No one will be able to repay your favors even if he bows to you respectfully, And offers you his hands or feet or anything else. No one will be able to repay your favors even if he carries you on his head or shoulders And respects you from the bottom of his heart for as many *kalpas* as there are sands in the River Ganges. Buddhism. Lotus Sutra 4

Qur'an 40.61,64: Cf. Qur'an 14.32-34, p. 310; 16.10-18,p. 141; 32.4-9,p.126; Wadhans, M.5,p.913. On gratitude to parents, see Qur'an 46.15-16,p.249. Lotus Sutra 4: The value of the Buddha's teaching is immeasurable. It touches eternity, which all temporal phenomena rolled up together cannot hope to attain. Hence no temporal acts of gratitude can possibly be worthy of it. Cf. Myokonin, p. 774

All human bodies are things lent by God. With what thought are you using them? Terrikyo. Ofudesaki 3.41

When a man is born, whoever he may be, there is born simultaneously a debt to the gods, to the sages, to the ancestors, and to men. When he performs sacrifice, it is the debt to the gods which is concerned. It is on their behalf, therefore, that he is taking action when he sacrifices or makes an oblation. And when he recites the Vedas it is the debt to the sages which is concerned. It is on their behalf, therefore, that he is taking action, for it is said of one who has recited the Vedas that he is the guardian of the treasure store of the sages. And when he desires offspring, it is the debt to the ancestors which is concerned. It is on their behalf, therefore, that he is taking action, so that their offspring may continue, without interruption. And when he entertains guests, it is the debt to man which is concerned. It is on their behalf, therefore, that he is taking action if he entertains guests and gives them food and drink. The man who does all these things has performed a true work; he has obtained all, conquered all. Hinduism, Satapatha Brahmana 1.7.2.1-5

Ah, children—Be not arrogant, but assist the deities of marvelous spirit power in their work. Even the grains, and the teeming grass and trees—Even these are favored with blessings from Amaterasu, Great Goddess of the Sun. Morning and evening, At each meal you take, consider the blessings of Toyouke-no-kami, you people of the world. The blessings of the Gods of heaven and earth—Without these, how could we exist, even for a day, even for a night? Satapatha Brahmana 1.7.2.4: On gratitude to one's parents, cf Anguttara Nikaya I.61,p. 250; Classic on Filial Piety 1, p.249. Ofudesaki 3.41: Cf. Sun Myung Moon, 9-30-79, p. 307. Filial obligation is a major topic in psychoanalysis.

Forget not the grace of generations of ancestors; From age to age, the ancestors are our own *ujigami*, Gods of our families. Father and mother are gods of the family; even so, honor them as gods with heartfelt service, all you of human birth.

Shinto. Norinaga Motoori, One Hundred Poems on the Jewelled Spear

One Hundred Poems on the Jewelled Spear; The *ujigami* are eponymous ancestors of the clan; one's ancestors should be reverenced. Toyouke-no-kami is the Good Goddess worshipped at the Outer Shrine of the Temple at Ise, and Amaterasu is the Sun Goddess; they represent all the productive forces of nature and humanity which provide our food.

We feel gratitude for these many gifts, and strive to return for what we have been given by spreading gratitude wherever we live.

If we spent more time working on our virtues, in addition to working to make money; working to improve our patience, working on our honesty, working on our gratitude, working on our education, working on our generosity and thoughtfulness, working at being kind, working on our family relations and working on our worship of our God, working on our social interest, and working out, we might work ourselves into greater freedom and becoming better human beings and living a happier and healthier life.

The Benefits of Gratitude

There are many wonderful events that happen to you when you live in the state of gratitude. First off, you find escape from the pains of negative thinking. Anger, envy, worries, jealousy, hatred and self pity are all connected in the ingrate state. When you lift up your heart and mind into the spiritual state of gratitude, you find an inner peace and constancy that spares you from the jarring events of the material world. With gratitude, you interpret life events into the gratitude state. You can train yourself to feel grateful that you are hungry, and feel grateful that you feel empty, and then you will feel grateful when you lose weight as your appetite comes under control. Yes, you can even feel gratitude when you lose your job, and get dumped, and when other misfortunes occur in your life. Many supposedly "bad" events can be interpreted into the state of gratitude where they lose their sting and seem less important. You will learn how to put the gratitude spin on every event in your life and find an unending source of events for which you will feel gratitude. The major benefit of this is a real deep inner peace, a place inside of yourself where you feel safe and good and life has new meaning when you are into gratitude. You always know what you are expecting when you are living in a state of gratitude. You are looking for and expecting a gratitude opportunity. You wait for something good to happen to you that will enhance and reinforce your experience of gratitude. You look for an opportunity to pay back for the many gifts you have been given. You put something back in for that and feel good about yourself for doing this, without grandiosity or inferiority. It's O.K. to express gratitude.

Material concerns, while still a bother, seem less threatening in the state of gratitude. You can deal with too much and too little with gratitude in your heart. As said in the fellowship, "you have to give it away to keep it: and thus it is with gratitude. Because of this, gratitude is a bridge back to society and instead of feeling superior and/or feeling ashamed, you can feel gratitude for the way you feel and for making your constructive contribution to society. The consistent interpretation of events into the gratitude state and paying back for what you have been given, leads to personal growth and the realization of your human spiritual potential. If you are religious, your gift is from your Higher Power or your God. Then you feel gratitude in your heart for what your Higher Power gave you, and strengthen your relationship with your Higher Power with acts of gratitude. Gratitude provides you with an inner locus of control from which you can lead a more constructive and loving life. For some earthly people, human gratitude may be the Higher Power.

The Points of Gratitude

Point 1. The first point is to live as much time as possible in the state of gratitude, saying thanks, and then taking action and putting a lot back in for what you have been given.

Point 2. Meditate and wonder about gratitude off and on all day long. Meditate for 5-10 minutes when you wake up. Meditate 2 minutes before and after you eat. Meditate for 5 minutes as you fill out your gratitude inventory in the morning and at night.

Point 3. The 3rd point of gratitude is to take your gratitude inventory and keep your inventory alive by recording three things that happened each day for which you feel gratitude.

Point 4. The fourth point of gratitude is to monitor your thoughts, feelings and actions to <u>detect errors of gratitude</u>—slipping into the ingrate state, and then correcting the error as soon as you can do so. Record times in the ingrate state in your gratitude inventory and describe how you converted out of the ingrate state into the mood of gratitude.

Point 5. The fifth point of gratitude is to publicly declare your gratitude, tell how it works for you and to put back in for what you have been given, happily, joyously and willingly.

Point 6. The sixth point of gratitude is to button down as many gratitude experiences as you can into your gratitude button so that buttoning your gratitude button puts you into a state of gratitude and takes you out of the ingrate states of violence, rage and anger.

Developing Gratitude

You set out to live a life of gratitude by seeing the events which occur in your life as gifts that have been given to you.

Yes, even some of the "bad" things that happen to you can be seen as gifts if you are determined to live gratitude. Strange as it may seem, you can feel gratitude for being fired from a job you love, or when losing a person you love, after being betrayed and/or being injured by the predators of your world.

Then you look for ways to say and do "Thank You," and put something back in for what you have been given. It is not uncommon for children who have lost a parent to death early on in their life, to become doctors and nurses and care

24

for the sick as a way of healing themselves, and pay back for the tragedy of the death of their parent in early life. This may sound naïve to those who live in revenge and negative thinking. I can only ask them, how does your head feel when it is loaded with hate and revenge and all the bad feelings that come from the negative view?

Keep your gratitude inventory every night and keep track of all the events in life you feel gratitude for.

It may be difficult to develop gratitude. Some may say it is anti-instinctual. One patient (psychotherapist) in my practice said that gratitude is a reaction formation to sadism. Gratitude can be contaminated by envy and oral sadistic impulses. But that is not the point. We utilize gratitude to counteract the agonies we inflict on ourselves with our envy, greed, hate and sadism. You need to work on your gratitude every day in every way in order for it to become internalized and real as a part of your life. You will cherish it and feel good about your gratitude. It is as easy to feel gratitude as it is to get angry and blame others and feel sorry for yourself because of all the injustices you have collected. Gratitude allows you to relate to what is, instead of cursing what isn't.

TEACHING THE GRATITUDE ATTITUDE

Dear Mr. Rosen,

Thank you very much for working so hard to organize the baseball league. I know you put a lot of time into it and I really appreciate your hard work making all the schedules and getting all the coaches. The uniforms were really cool. I hope we can have the league again next year.

Sincerely, Joey Diamond

This was the only note Mr. Rosen received after organizing the baseball league for 50 neighborhood boys. Sure, he got a bunch of verbal thank you's, but Joey was the only one who took the time to write a note.

Why is Joey different? He has a mother who thought about how to raise an appreciative child and trained her son to write notes.

When he was too young to write he drew a picture and his Mom helped him with the words. Now at the end of the school year, Joey writes thank you notes to his teachers. He includes in each note one thing he especially appreciated about this particular teacher (she cracks good joke) and one think he appreciated being taught (the unit on reptiles). Joey also writes notes at the end of the summer vacation to his camp counselors.

His counselor invited him to go swimming with him one day after camp was over so that he could learn how to dive. His first grade teacher told him she still has the note he sent her. And when the head of his baseball league had an extra ticket to a Dodgers game, guess which kid he called?

With all this positive feedback, Joey enjoys writing these notes. He is learning that people like to be appreciated, an important component of building healthy relationships.

IT DOESN'T HAPPEN ON ITS OWN

How many times have you said in exasperation, "This kid has no appreciation for a thing I do?"

If you have ever felt this way about your children, ask yourself, "What have I done to instill the trait of appreciation in them? Have I actually thought of a game plan to teach this trait or do I expect that somehow it will materialize on its own?"

Appreciating others is a skill that anyone can learn. Children can be taught to look more carefully at those around them and to focus on the many benefits they receive from them.

Ideally, parents should start with very young children, helping them to notice details and pointing out all the good that people do in general. This also teaches children to have what we call in Hebrew and *ayin tov*, a good eye.

When kids are encouraged to look for the good in others, even (and especially!) those they don't particularly like, they become more positive individuals who can find something nice to say about most anyone.

If we don't want our kids to be critical and negative, we need to realize that we have tremendous power to create the opposite.

TEACHING TIPS

Train your children to write thank you notes at an early age. They can write to teachers, counselors, coaches, anyone who gives them gifts (including grandparents) or the family friend who takes him to the circus.

Notes are important because they demonstrate and instill a higher level of appreciation. You have to think a lot more about what the person actually did for you since you want to write more than one line—you have to fill the page! Help your child notice the details.

Before bed, ask your child to name two things he or she appreciated today. (This will work best with younger children; you may get weird looks if you try this with your teen, but better late than never!) Then you share two things you appreciated. Be sure to include things the child did, such as putting something away, asking a good question or waiting patiently for something. Talking about what you appreciate about each other will help you build your relationship with your child as well.

Have a "Family Appreciation Meeting" at dinner one night a month, perhaps on a Friday evening. Go around the table and have everyone say one thing he or she appreciated about each member of the family that month.

Be a role model for your children. If you could use a little help in the appreciation department yourself, then you can't expect your children to be overflowing with gratitude. Start writing notes and pointing out all the good that people do for you. Thank the mailman and the garbage men. Say out loud, "Whatever would we do without the garbage men! Do you know how awful it would be if they didn't come every week!" Just because someone is paid to do a job doesn't mean we shouldn't thank them.

Help your child see a positive trait in someone he dislikes. Don't do it in the heat of the moment when he is telling you how much he hates his teacher. Teach him that everyone has good points to appreciate and that it's important to consciously look for them.

Point out wherever you go, all the good that you see people doing: highway workers who help us have a smooth ride, doctors and dentists who take care of us, cleaners who get out a nasty stain. There are so many people who help make life easier and more pleasant for us!

People are not naturally appreciative. We can't be annoyed with our children for being ungrateful if we have not taught them how to get into the "gratitude attitude".

Chana Heller, MSW, is the mother of five children, ages 10-18. She works for Aish HaTorah Los Angeles as the Coordinator of Student Services and has taught Jewish parenting Workshops for 8 years. She is married to Rabbi Dob Heller, also of Aish HaTorah LA

THE PRACTICE OF GRATITUDE
By Dewain Beigard

The following article was published in abbreviated form in the Mindfulness Bell—the journal of the Order of Interbeing (Tiep Hien). The full-length version is provided here in response to several requests.

St Paul wrote in closing his first letter to the Thessalonians, "En panti eucharistate" (In pahn-tee you-car-in-STAY-te) The King James Version translates this: "In everything, give thanks."

"Panti" is a form of the Greek word "pas." Literally it means "all." In English we meet it most often in the form "pan" as in Pan-African or Pan-American. It can refer to all things, all places, all situations, or the whole of something. In this saying of St. Paul I think "panti" is best translated "all circumstances."

Eucharisteite" is a form of the verb "eucharisteo." In this saying of St. Paul, I think it's best translated "be grateful." A noun derived from this same verb is used to name the central act of Christian practice: the Eucharist (also known as Communion or the Lord's Supper."

The practice of gratitude was clearly of great importance to early Christians. No so clear is that practicing gratitude can be a way of practicing mindfulness. One of the meanings listed in my Greek lexicon for the verb "eucharisteo" and its related forms is "mindful of benefits." I think St. Paul used this word to advise the Thessalonians that in all circumstances, no matter how negative, they should be mindful of those elements of joy and blessing that may also be present.

Every set of circumstances has both positive and negative dimensions, but the negative often predominates and threatens to overwhelm us. There is so much pain around us that most of us learn from an early age to harden our hearts to it— to shut out awareness of suffering. A paradox I have discovered in the practice of gratitude is that my capacity to be aware of suffering has increased in direct proportion to my capacity to experience joy and to be mindful of the blessings of every situation.

I think this is because compassion and joy are inseparable. Compassion and joy are two of the Four Holy Abodes of the Buddhas—the other two being loving-kindness and impartiality. All four of the Holy Abodes are interdependent and inseparable. In the Pali language, the word karuna (kuh-roo-NAH) is used to name compassion or mindfulness of suffering and the word mudita (moo-dih-TAH) is used to mean mindfulness of joy and happiness. One of these cannot be developed apart from the other.

One of the reasons I think our contemporary culture is so hedonistic is that many of us have not developed the capacity to experience pleasure and joy in a profound way. As the Rolling Stones say in one of their songs: "I try and I try and I try and I try—but I can't get no satisfaction." And I wonder if we will have much chance to develop our capacity to experience joy, happiness, and satisfaction very deeply so long as we are afraid to confront the suffering and pain around us and within us.

Even in our meditation practice, I've noticed we sometimes set up a duality that opposes mindfulness of the suffering around us to the mindfulness of joyful, happy and refreshing things. We may feel guilty when we enjoy our food, for instance, because we fear such pleasure will distract us from awareness of the hunger so prevalent in our world. On the other hand, we may pull back from a very deep awareness of such widespread hunger for fear of being overwhelmed and paralyzed by sadness.

But the issue of practice before us is not whether we should focus attention on the positive rather than the negative aspects of life or vice versa. The positive and negative dimensions of life are inseparable. If we harden our hearts to the pain around us and close our eyes to suffering, we also cut off our capacity to experience joy and happiness. And if we are not continually mindful of the joyful and beautiful elements of life, we cut off our capacity for compassion as well. For the benefit of all beings, therefore, we should consider it our responsibility to be mindful of the blessings and joys of every situation.

Sometimes we may find it difficult to see anything for which to be grateful in a particular situation. But even in the most miserable of circumstances, I've found comfort in some words of Meister Eckhart: "Remember this," he said, "All suffering comes to an end." We can at least be grateful for that.

Some years ago, a dear friend of mine named Jim, my life companion for many years, was lying sick in the Veteran's Hospital in New Orleans. One day he told me he could no longer get to the toilet and asked if I would help him with the bed pan. I was overjoyed at the opportunity to help. He wanted me to spend the night with him, because he was embarrassed to ask the nurse or orderly to help him with personal hygiene.

I called the physician and asked her permission to stay in the hospital with him. After some reluctance she agreed to grant me a pass to spend the night. It was about one thirty in the afternoon. I told Jim I would go home to take care of our dogs and cats and that I would return about seven o'clock. He asked me to fix his watch on a nearby shelf so he could tell the time. So I arranged his watch. Then I kissed him good-bye and left.

When I returned about six thirty, Jim appeared to be asleep. He was lying on his side in a position where he could see his watch, but his eyes were closed. His facial expression was peaceful. Then I noticed how still he was, and as I drew closer I realized that he was dead. I think he tried to hold on to life until seven o'clock when he knew I would return. But he wasn't able to hold on long enough.

For several days I could hardly stop crying. I cried myself to sleep at night. I even cried in my dreams. I woke up in the morning crying. But with the help of friends, I began to see how fortunate we were that Jim had been spared a long agonizing death. I realized firsthand the truth of a saying that had long been one of my favorite proverbs: "The power of love is greater than the power of death."

I feel truly blessed to have known Jim and to have shared so many years with him. His life continues to this day in many wonderful ways. He designed and built, for instance, the room in which our New Orleans Sangha meets.

In the years since that time, I have come to see, especially with the help of Thay Nhat Hanh's teachings, that for me the practice of gratitude in all circumstances is a fundamental and indispensable practice.

I know that nearly everyone of you can recount experiences similar to mine of pain, grief, and loss. Life is at times difficult for us all. In the Pali language, the word dukkha (kook-huh) which is often translated "suffering," in its root sense means "difficult." Life is dukkha. That is the First Noble Truth. Though it may seem paradoxical, dear friends, that truth is why I find it so necessary to practice St. Paul's advice to the Thessalonians. En panti, eucharisteite! In all circumstances, be grateful

http://ourworld.compuserve.com/homepates/Blue_Iris_Sangha/gratitud.htm
12/21/2000

Gratitude Moments

If the only prayer you ever say in your entire life is thank you, It will be enough.

Meister Eckhart

Beginning The Day With Gratitude

"If you focus on what you have, you'll end up having more. If you focus on what you lack, you will never have enough. That is a guarantee. I'm hoping that you will learn to take this to heart as I have and do as we are doing today. We are celebrating gratitude and really trying to (inspire) a shift in the consciousness in this country. And the shift in the country comes with each one of you who hears me today, a different way of looking at your life, being thankful for what you have and you will always end up having more. If you concentrate on what you don't have, you will never, ever have enough."

—Oprah Winfrey

You can use any type of journal you would like (even a notepad will do) and begin to record five things each and every day that you are thankful for in that day. Looking for those five things throughout the day and recording them will have an enormously positive impact on the way you view your life.

—Oprah Winfrey

Gratitude Reflection

We live in a culture
that puts its focus
on what we do not have
instead of the bounty
that flourishes about us.

It will take
a great deal of diligence
to teach ourselves
the art of gratitude.

Practice each day,
each hour,
each minute.
Notice and send
your prayer
of gratitude
for each blessing.

Oprah Winfrey

You also need to inventory your ingrate state. You need to describe your ingrate thoughts and actions and then how you transformed yourself into the attitude of gratitude.

Rachel, Roseanne and Billy Graham Gratitudes

My Gratitude Moment...Rachel's Gratitude Moment

In today's gratitude moment, I would like to say that I am grateful for Oprah.

For her teachings, for the wisdom she passes on to me, for the strength
She gives me every day, for the inspiration she gives me to succeed,
For the courage she gives me to strive for the best in life...

I am grateful for Oprah's parents for having her.

I am grateful for my television, the tool with which I can receive Oprah's
Teachings every day.

Have you had your gratitude moment today?

Roseanne shared her gratitude journal with Oprah...

I'm grateful that God exists and that I'm made of the same stuff.

I'm grateful that God gave me a way to turn some terrible things
into positive things so that I could grow.

I'm grateful, above all else, that I have raised moral children who
want to make the world better.

I'm grateful for my husband who has ethics and values that encourage
and inspire me.

I'm grateful for poets and friends and chocolate

...and America and comedians and double-extra-large sized clothing

...and Barbara Streisand, and Lenny Bruce, and Oprah, and the Simpsons

My strong body...brave heart...my ranch...my love of my work...my

33

religion, Judaism, and the Kabbalah, with all the mysteries that are so awesome and so fun for me to think about.

Have you had your gratitude moment today?

Oprah asked Billy Graham to share some of the things he is most grateful for in his life...

I'm most grateful that God has revealed Himself to us and that He's
Not sitting way out there in darkness but He's with us and can come
Into our hearts and lives and make a big difference.

I think Oprah's having this emphasis that I've heard so much about
is having a great impact on the country and I'm thankful for Oprah and
what she's been doing with this emphasis on thankfulness...and it's
not just Thanksgiving, it's every day of the year and that we need to
be thankful.

I'm most grateful for the great spiritual impact God has made in my
life and in my marriage; our marriage has been successful because
there's been three of us. There's been Ruth, me and God—and God
first, because if you leave God, or leave the spiritual out of your marriage,
I don't have much hope for your future.

Write down five instances of acting in the ingrate state today.

Write down five instances of how you converted your thoughts and actions from the ingrate state into the attitude of gratitude.

Write down five instance of feeling gratitude and putting something back in for what you have been given. Do gratitude five times and grow in gratitude (GIG).

Gratitude Grows Into Happiness
By Annie Zaleszek

OPRAH WINFREY keeps a Gratitude Journal. At the end of each day, she takes a moment to reflect upon those things in her life for which she is grateful. She writes down at least five. It's important to write them down, she says, because just thinking about it doesn't do it. Do what, I wondered?

After analyzing the idea, I decided there must be some legitimate merit to a practice that someone like Oprah Winfrey faithfully subscribes to. Oprah is a woman who has over-come the challenges of personal trauma in childhood, broken through major societal barriers and evolved into a woman of immense achievement. People around the world stand in awe of the success she has cultivated from ordinary and what many may possibly deem as disadvantaged circumstances.

If there is anyone who has things to be grateful for, it's Oprah. And if a Gratitude Journal works for Oprah, it can work for me. In a respectably hard-covered journal, every night I begin to write each of at least five points, beginning with "I am grateful for..."

I've been doing this for a while now, and I'm convinced of its value. But you be the judge...

Examine for yourself the life of anyone who has attained a level of measurable success and who is also considerably and obviously happy with him/herself. You will find, underlying their perceptions of what they've done and what they have, is a deep and peaceful sense of gratitude.

The gratitude may be towards people, incidents, a product, or a Supreme Being. To whom or what the gratitude is expressed does not seem to matter; the key is expression. Happy and successful people always make sure to acknowledge those people, events and things that have helped them arrive at their present status. Please don't confuse this with humility. Humility shuns the Self for the sake of others.

Gratitude is a far grander thing. Gratitude Celebrates Every One and Every Thing. Gratitude validates the purpose and mission of even the tiniest speck of Any Thing.

The act of expressing gratitude perpetuates a sense of love of all things created. Gratitude brings forth possibilities for further magnificent manifestations. Stop and think for a moment. Look around. Pick one thing, just one, for which you are grateful. It may be a material object you've recently acquired; it could be the sweet smile of a child that you are witnessing; you may be most grateful for a circumstance you were privileged to experience today. Tell yourself why you are grateful for this one particular thing. Come up with reasons to back it up.

For example: this object has enhanced my lifestyle; that smile made my heart grow with compassion; those circumstances brought me useful knowledge that will increase my business. Genuinely appreciate everything that has come about or may yet evolve as a result of this thing for which you are recognizing gratitude. Put your entire attention on the advantages you have already attained by having this thing in your life. Feel the gratitude course through your veins. Imagine it in every cell of your body.

Write down what you are grateful for and why. Now, having done all this, tell me honestly: what emotion are you experiencing? Does it feel like happiness? Maybe even love? Gratitude precedes happiness. Moreover, you can have instant happiness just by finding something to be grateful for. There is always something to be grateful for. Even in the darkest hour, though you may have to open your eyes a little wider, you will find something. Focus on it exclusively, and it will grow. It has to. It has no choice. Your mind has the choice. You are the director of your attention. Attend to that for which you are grateful. Your thoughts are seeds.

Your gratitude nourishes them like water and sunshine. Happiness will blossom and flourish. Gratitude is what does it. Just ask Oprah! Say it, write it, feel it, show it. Mean it. When the feeling of gratitude resonates through your being, you will not be able to avoid the inevitability of a wave of the "warm fuzzies" all over!

Written by Annie Zaleszsak, a writer and illustrator in Calgary, Alberta, Canada

Gratitude

http://www.fablesinverse.mcmail.com/Verses/gratitude.htm

A young lad,

One day, to school, on his way

Heard some loud squawking nearby.

By a verge of sedge in a thorny hedge

Was a crow which could not fly.

It could not take wing, or from the hedge spring,

So it squawked in loud protest

With one deft throw, his coat's over the crow.

Presence of mind at its best.

"Heh! Don't peck me." Spoke the schoolboy, Lee

Removing his coat from her.

The crow did a hop; then flew just a jot.

Then, up, up into the air.

Up into the sky; Lee looked at it, high,

As he continued his walk.

Crow veered in a back, approached on the flank

Zooming past with grateful squawk.

Crow watched the way of his friend each day;

Gave a squawk en route to school.

And Crow hung about till Lee's class was out.

Also homewards, as a rule.

One day a man tried to offer a ride

To Lee on his homeward route.

With wide open door, he seemed to implore.

Lee, in turn, deemed to refute.

The mans insistence, and Lee's resistance

Seemed to Crow on high a threat

Down, down he swooped, around the man looped

Attacking his face and head

Thus well defeated the man retreated

While Lee, escaping, ran home.

Told Mum, "I know. I was saved by my crow."

She told the police, by phone.

Lee's kindness to aid was truly repaid.

Between boy and bird, a bond.

'Twas its way to talk, our crow and his squawk.

At which Lee waved, ever fond.

No Styx WoW as this is a modern fable by the author.

Everyday should be a day of thanksgiving on the Christian's calendar!
    We are taught by command to be grateful
    We are taught by example to be thankful. Jesus was thankful
How to obtain a grateful heart (spirit)
        Remember never to forget
        Do not major on your troubles
        Think how much better off you are than so many others
        Count the blessings you do have rather than concentrating on what you
        do not have
        Consider how detestable ingratitude really is
        Express your gratitude
        Do not take the commonplace things of life for granted

Avoid overemphasizing the luxuries of life
Do away with murmuring and complaining
Realize that you are a recipient, and never forget the giver of the gift.

It is the will of God that we be thankful!! I Thess.5:18

We must do the will of God to enter the Kingdom of Heaven. Matt 7:21

Even Christ had to do the will of the Father—John 4:34; 5:19; 5:30; 6:38; 8:28

Thus gratitude is NOT OPTIONAL!
To be an ingrate is to be disobedient; and to be disobedient is to BE LOST!
Jesus was thankful. Matt 11:25; 26:27; Mark 8:6; John 11"41—and He is our example!
David—I Chron. 16:7-36; Ps 100.
Paul—Acts 27:35; 28:15' Phil 1L3; 4:6
Anna—Luke 2:38
Daniel—Daniel 6:10
All had thankful hearts.
The Angelic host gives thanks! Rev. 7:11,12

1. Remember to never forget

"Forget not all His benefits." Psalms 103:2 Forgetfulness is a foe of gratitude.
Though Joseph befriended him, the butler forgot him! Gen. 40:23
Only one of the ten lepers remembered to thank God. Lk. 17:11.

2. Do not major on your troubles

Count your blessings not your bruises. How often do we major on our troubles rather than our blessing? We even date matters from a tragedy. A year ago today the tornado blew our house away or that was the year I almost died of the flu. If we are not careful while we walk the pathway of life we will never pluck a rose, but will pluck many thorns and wear them in our hearts! Lets not major in troubles!

In fact we should be grateful even for our troubles and so called inconveniences. One little boy was thankful for his glasses, for they kept the boys from fighting him and the girls from kissing him! Matthew Henry wrote in his diary upon his house being robbed:

"Let me be thankful first, because he: Never robbed me before
Because although he took my purse he did not take my life.
It was not much. Because it was I who was robbed not I who robbed!
All things work together for good to them that love God." Romans 8:28

Think how much better off you are than so many!

3. Count the blessings you do have rather than concentrating on what you do not have.

"And having food and raiment let us be there with content." I Timothy 6:8
"Be content with such things as ye have." Hebrews 13:5

So often we fail to remember the things with which we are so blessed. A mother and father gave a sizable gift to the church in memory of their son who was killed in WW2. When the gift was announced, a mother whispered to her husband, "Let's give the same amount for our boy." The husband replied, "Our son didn't lose his life." The mother replied, "THAT'S THE POINT! Let us give is as an expression of gratitude for sparing his life." This mother had not lost sight of the fact of what she did have!!

How often we sing, but how seldom we practice. "Count your many blessing name them one by one, and it will surprise you what the Lord has done:

a. We should try and count our spiritual blessings Eph. 1:3
   There God's son, the incomparable church, the Holy Bible, the exceeding and great and precious promises, the sustaining hope of heaven, our conversion, and so on and so on.
b. We should try and count our physical blessings. There are our families, our health, our food, shelter and clothing, our freedom, the beauty of the world, and so on.
   We will come to see that these blessings are innumerable.

4. Consider how detestable ingratitude really is.

"Neither were thankful" Romans 1:21 is one of the many sins on the black and vicious list of sins characteristic of the Gentile world. Too, in describing the perilous times of the last days, along with many other tragic transgressions, Paul says men will be "unthankful." II Timothy 3:1-

5. Indeed, God reckons ingratitude so DETESTABLE as to catalog it with the most vicious vices and the most tragic of transgressions. Shakespeare said in "As You Like It."
"Blow, blow thou winter wind, thou are not so unkind as man's ingratitude."

6. Express your gratitude

   Express your gratitude verbally. We are instructed to "give" thanks; not "feel" or "think" thanks. I Thess.5:18; Eph.5:20. "O give thanks unto the Lord, for He is good...Let the redeemed of the Lord say so..." Ps. 107:1,2

   Weary and burdened with the cares of the day, the preacher's little girl came into his study, climbed into his lap, and said, "Daddy I did not come to ask for a thing. I just came to tell you I love you." The statement so warmed the heart of the preacher that his weariness was soon forgotten. In like manner, God is the Father and He desires and longs for His children to express their love and gratitude.

   Express our gratitude by your life as well as by our lips. Thanks saying is NOT necessarily thanks giving, but thanks living is! In response to David's question, "What shall I render unto the Lord for all His benefits toward me?" Ps. 116:12. Let us all resolve that we will give unto God our love, our time, our talents, our money, our lives, our ALL!

7. Do Not Take the Commonplace Things of Life For Granted

   We are so thankless because we are so thoughtless. Think and thank come from the same root word. And, in our thinking, it is so easy to let the commonplace and ordinary blessings of life be forgotten and unappreciated. For example, if the sun did not rise one day we would all be frantic; but what about the many days year after year the sun does rise? Do we daily stop to think that such takes place by the grace of God; and then, pause and thank Him for the same? Too, it is so easy for us to take our everyday material blessings for granted. For example, because of the appliances and conveniences, such as radios, televisions, computers, cell phones, electrical lights, automatic washer and dryers, VCRs, CD players, DVD players, and many others.

8. Avoid Overemphasizing the Luxuries of Life.

   We must understand that "a man's life consisteth not in the abundance of the things which he possesseth." Luke 12:15
   We must be thankful for the simple necessities:

"They huddled inside the storm door, two children in ragged, outgrown coats. "Any old papers, lady?" I was busy. I wanted to say no, until I looked down at their feet. Their little sandals covered with sleet. "Com in and I'll make you a cup of hot cocoa." I woman said. There was no conversion. Their soggy sandals left marks upon the hearthstone. Cocoa and toast with jam to fortify against the chill outside. I went back to the kitchen and started again on my household budget. The silence in the front room struck through to me. I looked in. The girl held her empty cup in her hands looking at it. The boy asked in a flat voice: "Lady, are you rich?" "Am I rich? NO!" I looked at my shabby slipcovers. The girl put cup back in its saucer carefully. "Your cups match your saucers," she said. Her voice was old, with a hunger that was not of the stomach. They left then, holding their bundles of papers against the wind. They hadn't said thank you. They didn't need to. They had more than that. Plain blue pottery cups and saucers. But, they matched. I tested the potatoes and stirred the gravy. Potatoes and brown gravy, a roof over our heads, my husband has a steady job these things matched, too. I moved the chairs back from the fire and tidied the living room. The muddy prints of small sandals were still wet on my hearth. I let them be. I want them in case I ever forget how rich I am. "Yes, we need to be thankful for slip covers, matching-blue-pottery-cups-and-saucers, potatoes-and-brown-gravy things of life!

We must be thankful for, and put the emphasis on, the spiritual things. Eph.1:3

An aged Christian was called upon by the tax assessor to determine the amount of taxes that he should pay. When asked what property he had, the aged Christian stated, "I am a very wealthy man." The tax assessor asked him to list his possessions. The aged man did.

I have a mansion in heaven-John 14:2

I have peace that passeth understanding-Phil.4:7

I have joy unspeakable-I Peter 1:8

I have a divine love that never faileth-I Cor. 13:8

I have a faithful, pious wife (conscientious in religious practices) Proverbs 31:10

I have devoted children-Exodus 20:12

I have true, loyal friends who sticks closer than a brother-Proverbs 18:24

I have songs in the night-Ps.42:8

I have a crown of life-James 1:12

I have remission of sins—Acts 2:38

I have a Saviour, Jesus Christ, who supplies all my needs freely-Phil. 4:19

Closing the book, the tax assessor said, "You are truly a wealthy man, but do you know that I am not able to tax you on any of this" He then added, "You have possessions that give you 100% profit."

You have been bought with a price. I Cor. 7:23

9. Do Away with Murmuring and Complaining

Instead of remaining continually grateful for their deliverance from Egypt, how soon did Israel start to murmur and complain? Exodus 15:24; 17:3 Num. 14:2
Let us avoid duplicating this spirit. I Cor. 10l:10. Though he was in prison at the time, Paul still penned, "Giving thanks always for all things." Eph. 5:20, and "Do all things without murmurings and disputings." Phil 2:14.

In The City of Happiness, Complaining Avenue and Thanksgiving Lane are miles apart, so that you cannot live on both streets at the same time. "Some people who should be humbly grateful only become more grumpy and hateful." Into which group do you fall?

10. Realize That You Are a Recipient; and Never Forget the Giver in the Gift

All that we have we received of God. James 1:17. Paul was so deeply conscious of this. I Cor. 14:10; Romans 1:5, whereas the rich farmer failed to realize the same. Luke 12:16-21 Now, let us never forget the giver in the gift. A child who has been pampered by an over-indulgent uncle forgets the candy. Why? The child is more interested in the gift than in the giver. It is possible for us to have the same attitude toward God. When God healed our sick loved one in the same attitude toward God. When God healed our sick loved one in answer to our prayers, and we forgot to give Him thanks, had we not forgot the giver in the gift? Were we not guilty in being interested in the blessings to the neglect of the blesser? The young bride-to-be is most grateful for her new engagement ring; but, she is much most grateful for her new engagement ring, but, she is more grateful for the one who gave it to her. Apart from him, the ring means nothing. Accordingly, let us never separate God from His gifts.

Our Father, Thou hast given us so much. Do, please, give us one more thing...a grateful heart!"

Scriptures
    Gen. 40:3
    Col.2"7; 3:15;4:2
    Eph. 1:3; 5:20
    I Thess. 5:18
    Mark 8:6
    John 11:41; 14:2
    I Peter 1:8; 2:21,22
    I Chron. 16:7-36
    Ps. 100; 103:2; 107:1,2; 116:12
    Daniel 6:10
    I Samuel 31:1-13; 11: 1-15
    Romans 1:5; 1:21; 8:28
    Hebrews 13:5
    Luke 2:38; 12:15; 17:11-19; 12:16-21
    Acts 2:38; 27:35; 28:15
    Rev. 7:11,12
    II Timothy 3:1-5
    Phil. 1:3; 4:6; 2:14; 4:7; 4:19
    Proverbs
    31:10; 18:24
    Exodus 5:20; 15:24; 17:3; 20:12
    James 1:12; 1:17
    Numbers 14:2

Giving thanks to God is mandatory* I Thess. 5:18; Eph. 5:20

The Ingrate State

Gratitude is a state of being, composed of spiritual, mental, emotional and physical components. The Ingrate State, or ingratitude, also is a complex state of being, with characteristic words and deeds. Various states of ingratitude have been described in the literature on addictive and mental disorders. Because there are so many variations on this theme it is only possible for me to allude to the more prevalent types of ingratitude and we will work out the details in time.

The central importance of malicious envy has been described by Melanie Klein in her work entitled "Envy and Gratitude." Reading this work, one can get an impression of the great destructive power of envy and wonder how you can possibly get over the envy state into the attitude of gratitude. Malicious envy arises out of the basic function of the nerve cells of the brain. The nerve cells that compose the brain are almost all difference detector neurons. They fire their electrical impulse when a difference in stimulation occurs on their dendrite endings. The whole of our thinking and feeling is built up into a map created by these differences. As we map out these differences into positions and sizes, we become impressed with high intensities and low intensities, and with large events and small ones. We are biologically cursed to detect differences and the very basis of our cognition, of our knowing the world, is the cause of hate, prejudice and the wish to attack and destroy those who are different from us. Envy is our blessing and our curse. Sad to say, there are very few similarity detector neurons in the brain. Our initial destructive envy is directed at the breast, according to Klein, and our subsequent relationships with others and our internal objects (maps of events in our world) derive from what happens to our envy. It is also the curse of those who dare to be different and successful and incite the ill will and envy of those less fortunate. Envy is the root of man's inhumanity to man. We play the fatal game of "Mine is better than yours".

The ingrate state is characterized by a failure in development of gratitude and the persistence of traits, thoughts and deeds associated with envy, and attempting to make others envious. The ingrate state is characterized by a lack of affiliation motives. The bipolar self of the ingrate is polarized between feeling superior and feeling inferior, between grandiosity and shame. As said in the AA fellowship, an alcoholic is a megalomaniac with an inferiority complex. "THE GREAT I AM" gives no credit to others, intends to be in control of others, and acts upon malicious envy in establishing superior pecking rights with weaker people. In Adlerian psychology, the infant is seen in a position of organic inferiority (it is smaller than adults) and strives for superiority to overcompensate for the feelings of inferiority, engendered by envy of the superior sized adults. Adolescents like to turn the table on adults and start performing adult like behaviors before they know the consequences of what they are doing. Their envy is their undoing. Melanie Klein's writing on psychoanalysis are couched in the strange language of that discipline, so I cannot explain what she has written to an uninitiated audience. She worked with words like splitting in the ego, projective identification and good and bad internalized objects in a complex way of conceptualizing how breast envy develops and interferes with gratitude. Her work is the basis for a current theory of "object relations" in psychoanalysis, and is clinically applied in the understanding and treatment of "borderline patients", who are among the most envious, hateful, explosive and difficult to manage people in the world. They are the very model of ingratitude.

The Ingrate State denies the gifts that have been given to the ingrate and denies connections with others, who are used and exploited for the selfish purposes of the ingrate. The ingrate does not recognize the rules that are made for us fools and so he lies, cheats, steals and breaks rules, laws, and limits with impunity. It is the ingrate's intention to manipulate others to pay the bills incurred by unethical and illegal actions. The Ingrate shirks responsibility and refuses to pay his/her bills and obligations. "Justice is when I get what I want when I want it" is the concept of the ingrate mentality. Therefore there is always blaming and finger-pointing and denial of personal responsibility. "Poor me" is an insincere game played by the ingrate in order to elicit sympathy from others and take advantage of them. "That's not fair" indicates that the ingrate did not get his (her) way, and society is supposed to jump to take care of the poor ingrate who has been "bum rapped."

The ingrate wants to be envied and to hurt other people by getting them to envy the ingrate. Thus the ingrate always is special, unique and different and finds ways to incite envy in others. Since this has to be done with little or no effort, the ingrate lies a lot and appears to be the greatest. This is helped by consuming incredible amounts of alcohol and drugs.

The ingrate does not feel thanks or appreciation for the gifts he (she) has been given. But mostly the ingrate will not show gratitude in action or pay back for what he (she) has received. This refusal to give, this refusal to offer of ones self, this refusal to work and put out energy, to "put something back in" for others or society is the hallmark of ingratitude. It has remarkable consequences in the life of the ingrate. It is the way the ingrate stays "cooled out" of society and ultimately the cause of the rejection of the ingrate by society family and friends. "Take, take, take" only goes so far. The refusal to give, called an "oral refusal" by some in the psychiatric community, is a tool the ingrate uses to get rejected.

He does not know that and thus always feels his rejections are undeserved. "I don't care" said with most vulgar words is the motto of the ingrate state.

The refusal to give causes a learning disability, for you have to put out a lot of work in order to learn and you do not get paid for that. The ingrate will not "put out" the effort required to learn. The ingrate comes up with excuses, blames, rationalizations, and lies to get out of work of any kind and especially schoolwork. The ingrate whines, It's too hard. I'm too little. I can't do it." This is the beginning of a life of negative thinking, that the ingrate uses to get out of doing work and putting forth the effort required to get the job done and finish it right.

Negative thinking is the curse of those who will not try, who will not do their best. It is a great convenience to think negative for it covers the ingrate's behind. "Poor me" is the name of the ingrate game. It's not fair. And envy rises up again and is focused on those who do get ahead because of a combination of luck, work and the fear of negative thinking and the feelings of shame that remain intact because of the inability or oral refusal to put something back in for what has been given. As Marlon Brando once noted, "I could of been a contenda" is the lament of the potential people who never achieved up to their level of ability because they refused to do the work and to put something back in, in return for what they have been given.

Noncompliance

Noncompliance seems to be the one link that unites everyone in the world. If the people who seek to lose weight follow my instructions, they lose weight and the process is wonderful, exciting and fulfilling. The ones who do not lose weight do not follow my instructions and do not lose weight. There are 10,000,000 reasons and excuses for not following instructions. They are all summed up in the word noncompliance. I ask my patients to read about Gunga Din, who followed instructions to the T and achieved his goal. But I think there was only one Gunga Din, and he is not one of my patients. My patients forget their medications, lose their medications, have a bird that knocks their medication down the sink, lose their purse with the medications in it, and leave their medications in San Francisco. They overeat because the Chicago Cubs win a game and because the Chicago Cubs lose a game. They overeat because they are at home too much and because they eat out too much. They lose their diet sheet, can't remember where they left their eating plan, feel that the maid stole their diet sheet, and feel so great that they have lost twenty five pounds that they were entitled to eat that piece of chocolate cake to celebrate their weight loss! My patients are sweet, charming, wonderful, brilliant, intelligent, clever, witty, negative thinking, frustrated and disappointed that they didn't lose all their weight in ten days, but above all else, they are non-compliant in the area of their love and addiction. It is as if we are all Thoreau and Emerson living on our own Walden Pond. "For nonconformity the world whips you in its displeasure," "Whoso would be a man would be a noncomformist. Trust thyself, every heart beats to that eternal string." My goodness. All right, already. Be a non-conformist and enjoy your obesity and fat. Why do you come to me to lose weight and then blow off all of my instructions and mock my suggestions? Oh my, you are so sly. Is there such a thing as unconscious ingratitude? You do not show your gratitude for the pretty face you were given at birth. You do not show your gratitude for your beautiful figures and ruined it at the fast food chains. Ah, pleasure. Sucker. What is the greater pleasure—a chocolate bar or a size eight dress and feeling proud of your face and figure. Why not both? Eat the candy bar and then diet. Or diet and then eat the candy bar. Do our impulses over-ride our gratitude or do we have a defect in gratitude and express our ingratitude in our impulsiveness and loss of control. You didn't know that loss of control awaits in the ingrate? Yes, it does. You can't control yourself because you have been into ingratitude for so long that it is you now. Only the practice of gratitude can pull you out of your noncompliance, because you and I know that you do not want to be out of control and get killed. Or is that your ultimate expression of defiance, noncompliance and ingratitude.

Taking Life for Granted

A young lady called me on the phone to ask for an appointment for the treatment of depression and bulimia. She was treated with Prozac by a doctor in Texas and wanted to know if I would prescribe the medication for her. I introduced the word gratitude into the conversation and she said she did not know much about it, did not know what that was and never felt it. I asked her if she felt grateful for her eyes and her ability to see the sunshine and flowers. She said she just took that for granted and did not see how appreciation entered into that. Then she seemed surprised by her answer. I asked her what she did appreciate and she said nothing, that she took it all for granted—even her $80,000 salary as a computer programmer, the friends she had, the associates she worked with and her teachers. I wondered out loud how a person could not feel grateful for their eyes and the visions of snow and flowers and trees. She said she took all that for granted. This lady also did not feel gratitude for her food which she also took for granted and she vomited it regularly with her lack of appreciation. As with many bulimic patients, the acid vomited up from her stomach had worn away the fillings in her teeth and she did not like that consequence either. What does a person have if they do not have gratitude and a feeling of appreciation for what they have? The bitter taste of hydrochloric acid and bile in the mouth.

A HISTORY OF AMERICAN INGRATITUDE

That's the trouble with directors. Always biting the hand that lays the golden egg.

~ Samuel Goldwyn

One ungrateful man does an injury to all who stand in need of aid.

~ Publilius Syrus

Ingratitude is treason to mankind.

~ James Thomson

Monte J. Meldman M.D.

The Elephant King Goodness
(Generosity and Ingratitude)

Once upon a time the Enlightenment Being was born as an elephant. He was wonderfully white in color, glowing like polished silver. His feet were as smooth and bright as the finest lacquer. His mouth was a red as the most elegant red carpet. And his marvelous eyes were like precious jewels, sparkling in five colors—blue, yellow, red, white and crimson.

The splendid beauty of this magnificent elephant was the outer form of the Enlightenment Being. But this was only a pale reflection of his inner beauty—Because during many previous lives he had filled himself with the Ten Perfections: energy, determination, truthfulness, wholesomeness, giving up attachment to the ordinary world, evenmindedness, wisdom, patience, generosity, and of course—loving kindness.

When he became an adult, all the other elephants in the Himalayan forests came to follow and serve him. Before long his kingdom contained a population of 80,000 elephants. Such a large nation was crowded and filled with distractions. In order to live more quietly, he separated himself from the rest and went to live alone in a secluded part of the forest. Because of his wholesomeness and purity, which were easily seen by everyone, he was known as the Elephant King Goodness.

The Elephant King Goodness heard the sound of the poor lost man's frightened weeping. Immediately he was filled with pity and compassion. Wishing to help him in any way he could, he began walking through the forest towards him.

But the man was in such a big panic that, when he saw the gigantic elephant coming towards him, he started running away. When the wise elephant king saw this, he stopped moving. Seeing this, the forester also stopped. Then King Goodness began walking towards him again, the man started running, and once again stopped when the elephant stopped.

At that point the man thought, "This noble elephant! When I run, he stops. And when I stop, he walks towards me. No doubt he intends me no harm-he must want to help me instead!" Realizing this gave him the courage to stop and wait.

As the Elephant King Goodness slowly approached, he said, "My human friend, why are you wandering about crying in panic?

50

"Lord Elephant," said the man, "I lost all sense of direction, became hopelessly lost, and was afraid I would die."

Then the Enlightenment Being took the forester to his own secluded dwelling place. He comforted and soothed him by treating him to the finest fruits and nuts in all the Himalayas. After several days he said, "My friend, don't be afraid. I will take you to the land where people live. Sit on my back." Then he began carrying him towards the land of men.

While riding comfortably on this glorious being, the man thought, "Suppose people ask me where I was. I must be able to tell everything." So he made notes of all the landmarks, while being carried to safety by the kind elephant king.

When he came out of the thick forest near the highway to Benares, the Elephant King Goodness said, "My good friend, take this road to Benares. Please don't tell anyone where I live, whether they ask you or not." With these parting words, the gentle elephant turned around and went back to his safe and secret home.

The man had no trouble finding his way to Benares. Then one day, while walking in the bazaar, he came to the shops of the ivory carvers. They carved ivory into delicate and beautiful statues, scenes and shapes. The forester asked them, "Would you buy tusks that come from living elephants?"

The ivory carvers replied, "What a question! Everyone knows the tusks from a live elephant are much more valuable than from a dead one." "Then I will bring you some live elephant tusks," said the forester.

Caring only for money, ignoring the safety of the elephant king, and without any gratitude towards the one who had saved his life—the man put a sharp saw in with his other provisions, and set out towards the home of King Goodness.

When he arrived the elephant king asked him, "Oh my dear human friend, what brings you back again?" Making up a story, the greedy man said, "My lord elephant, I am a poor man, living very humbly. As these times are very difficult for me, I have come to beg from you just a little piece of tusk. If you can give it to me, I will take it home and sell it. Then I will be able to provide for myself, and survive for a while longer."

Pitying the man, the Elephant King Goodness said, "Of course my friend, I will give you a big piece of tusk! Did you happen to bring a saw with you?"

"Yes, lord," said the forester, "I did bring a saw." "All right then," said the generous King Goodness, "but from both my tusks!"

The Enlightenment Being picked up both pieces with his trunk. He said, "Good friend, I am not giving you my lovely tusks because I dislike them and want to get rid of them. Nor is it because they are not valuable to me. But a thousand times, even a hundred thousand times more lovely and valuable are the tusks of all knowable wisdom, which leads to the realization of all Truth."

Giving the wonderful tusks to the man, it was the elephant's wish that his perfect generosity would eventually lead him to the greatest wisdom.

The man went home and sold both pieces of ivory. But it didn't take long for him to spend all the money. So again he returned to the Elephant King Goodness. He begged him, "My lord, the money I got by selling your ivory was only enough to pay off my debts. I am still a poor man, living very humbly. Times are still hard in Benares, so please give me the rest of your tusks, oh generous one!"

Without hesitation, the elephant king offered what was left of his tusks. The man cut off all that he could see of them, right down to the sockets in the elephant's skull! He left without a word of thanks. The wonderful kind elephant meant no more to him than a bank account! He took the ivory back to Benares, sold it, and squandered the money as before.

Once again the forester returned to the Himalayan home of the Elephant King Goodness. And again he begged him, "Oh noble elephant king, it is so very hard to make a living in Benares. Have pity on me and let me have the rest of your ivory—the roots of your tusks."

Perfect generosity holds nothing back. So once again the elephant king bent down on his knees and offered his remaining stumps of ivory. The ungrateful betrayer did not care at all for the elephant. He stepped onto the magnificent trunk—like a thick silver chain. He climbed up and sat between the pure white temples on top of the great head—like a snowy Himalayan dome. Then he roughly dug in with his heels, rubbing and tearing away the tender flesh from the stumps of the once-beautiful tusks. He used his dull worn-down saw to cut and hack the ivory roots out of the noble skull.

It is said there are many worlds—the hell world of torture, the worlds of hungry ghosts, of animals and of mankind, as well as many heaven worlds—from the lowest to the highest. In all these worlds there are millions of beings who, at one time or another, have been born and lived as elephants. And some who tell this story say, that although they knew not why, all those one-time elephants felt the pain of the Great Being—the Elephant King Goodness.

The forester departed carrying the bloody ivory stumps. Thinking there was no reason to see the elephant again, he didn't bother to show any sign of gratitude or respect.

The vast solid earth, which is strong enough to easily support great mountains, and is able to bear the worst filth and stench, could not bear and support this cruel man's enormous unwholesomeness. So, when he could no longer be seen by the suffering elephant, the mighty earth cracked open beneath him. Fire from the lowest hell world leaped up, engulfed him in bright red flames, and pulled him down to his doom!

The moral is: The ungrateful stops at nothing, and digs his own grave.

http://www.buddhanet net/bt 19.htm

I hate ingratitude more in a man than lying, vainness, babbling, drunkenness, or any taint of vice whose strong corruption inhabits our frail blood.
                                                                              Twelfth Night.

PAIN
By Kahil Gibran

Your pain is the breaking of the shell that encloses your understanding.

Even as the stone of the fruit must break, that its heart may stand in the sun, so must you know pain.

And could you keep your heart in wonder at the daily miracles of your life, your pain would not seem less wondrous than your joy;

And you would accept the seasons of your heart, even as you have always accepted the seasons that pass over your fields.

And you would watch with serenity through the winters of your grief.

Much of your pain is self-chosen.

It is the bitter potion by which the physician within you heals your sick self.

Therefore trust the physician, and drink his remedy in silence and tranquility:

For his hand, though heavy and hard, is guided by the tender hand of the Unseen.

And the cup he brings, though it burn your lips, has been fashioned of the clay

which the Potter has moistened with His own sacred tears.

> "On Pain" from THE PROPHET by Kahlil Gibran
> Alfred A. Knopf, 1982, New York

Does your gratitude match your pain? Can your gratitude overcome your pain? The cup is filled with gratitude. His own sacred tears are His gift to your Gratitude. Love Monte.

Shakespeare's Monsters of Ingratitude

At the very start of his sufferings, Lear cries out, 'Monster Ingratitude!' (I.v.37) and ingratitude, Sir Thomas Elyot writes, is 'commonly called unkindness.' (1) Shakespeare uses 'unkindness' about as frequently as he uses 'ingratitude' (2) Now, 'unkind' means cruel because cruel people are not being true to their (human/e) nature (kind), and that means they are being 'unnatural,' which is true of the 'monster' and all things 'monstrous', extensions of the same reality. The task of the following pages is to examine the articulation and interplay of these words as they occur in various plays by Shakespeare. But first, what is meant by 'ingratitude'? And why is it considered so 'monstrous'?

In *As You Like It,* Amiens sings one of Shakespeare's best-known songs:

> Blow, blow, thou winter wind
> Thou art not so unkind
> As man's ingratitude
> Thy tooth is not so keen,
> Because thou art not seen,
> Although thy breath be rude...

Freeze, freeze, thou bitter sky,
That dost not bite so nigh
As benefits forgot
Thought thou the waters warp,
Thy sting is not so sharp
As friend remember'd not...(II.vii.174ft)

In Shakespeare the winter is described (in various plays) as 'rough, angry, frozen, churlish, barren, biting, and furious': terribly cruel then, bringing suffering especially to the defenseless poor. Yet, the song says, ingratitude is more 'unkind' than winter. Very unkind indeed, in that case. But do we today think of ingratitude as such a terrible 'cruelty'? For English-speaking people now, 'ingratitude' implies little more than impolite behavior; not even muttering a 'thank-you'.

The song in *As You Like It* offers two precise examples of the behavior it calls 'ingratitude': 'benefits forgot' and 'friend remember'd not': In *Richard III* Dorset offers another definition:

In common worldly things, 'tis call'd ungrateful
With dull unwillingness to repay a debt
Which with a bounteous hand was kindly lent (II.ii.91-ff)

and we may compare this with modern definitions: '(not) showing or feeling gratitude' (The Concise Oxford Dictionary). Obviously, the plays suggest, a person's feelings will only be recognized on the basis of the actions which express them, unlike the winter's wind, actions of ingratitude are 'seen', because they are done. Yet, at the same time, ingratitude is an absence, a negation: it is that which is not done, not remembered; cause and effect, then, action and inaction, all bear the same name.

Shakespeare uses 'ingratitude' twenty times altogether, in thirteen plays (as opposed to only four uses of 'gratitude!'. Four times he uses the word 'unthankfulness', including the Friar's cry in *Romeo and Juliet:* 'O deadly sin, O rude unthankfulness'(III.iii.24),while 'unthankful' is found once. He never employs 'ungratefulness', found several times in Sidney (A&S 31 'Do they call Vertue there ungratefulnesse?') and probably originally coined by him (3) the form 'ungrateful' is used only six times in *A Midsummer Night's Dream* Helena cries, 'Injurious Hermia! Most ungrateful maid'(III,ii, 195) before she relates the past history of their friendship, which brings us back to Amiens' 'friend forgot'—she even asks 'O, is all forgot?' (line 201). We find the strongest language in an example not surprisingly from *Timon of Athens.*

O, see the monstrousness of man
When he looks out in an ungrateful shape (III.ii.74-5).

The shape is that of Lucius who refuses to help Timon in his time of need, after he had received much from him in the past (Dorset's 'dull unwillingness to repay a debt'). The First Stranger makes the remark; and the Second adds "Religion groans at it'. To be ungrateful, or unthankful, then, is an action against the natural order, and against the divine order too; that was also suggested by the Friar's 'deadly sin' seen above. Then in contrast 'gratitude' seems to be a requirement of natural law itself.

In Shakespeare's texts, the forms 'ingrate', ingrateful', and ingratitude' are used some forty times in all. As for the variants 'ungrateful/ingrateful', it seems that Shakespeare prefers the form ingrateful', perhaps on account of the strength given by a closer link to the word 'ingratitude'. That ingratitude is a strong word, we can deduce from such lines as 'ingratitude, Which Rome reputes to be a heinous sin' (*Titus Andronicus* I/i.447-8), and Lear's 'Ingratitude, thou marble-hearted fiend' *(King Lear* I.iv.257). Clearly, a quasi-religious feeling of outrage is provoked by ingratitude, which Lear expresses:

All the stor'd vengeances of Heaven fall
On her ingrateful top! (II.iv.159-60)

Ingratitude, he suggests, invites nothing less than heavenly wrath as punishment.

In about 1439 Lydgate wrote in his *Fall of Princes:*

For of al vicis, shortli to conclude, Werst of alle is ingratitude. (III 718.1651-2) 4)

(4) This is the 'proverb' listed by Tilley (5) and Dent (6) as 166: 'Ingratitude comprehends (is the worst of) all faults (vices)'. The words found in Lydgate are not a new expression invented by him, but rather represent the first recorded echoing in English of a Latin 'tag', which we find quoted in George Gascoigne's *The Glasse of Government* (1575): "I did often tymes defend in Schooles this proposition. *Ingratitudo (tam versus Deos immortales quam apud homines) peccatum maximum',* which is found in English in a later passage of the same work: 'as ingratitude is the most heinous offence against God, so have I taught you that it is the greatest fault in humayne actions' (Dent, PLED p.439 166).

These examples show that there has been a considerable change in the relative weight attached to 'ingratitude'; for who today, asked which was the worst possible form of human behaviour, the worst sin or vice, would name ingratitude? We must therefore be attentive when the word occurs in Shakespeare, because we may easily trivialize it, and not feel the full depth of moral shock, even religious horror, provoked by its denied obligations.

The question now must be why ingratitude is so terrible a thing, the worst of all vices and offenses? 'Benefits forgot, 'friend remember'd not,' said Amiens' song. Ingratitude, we may say, is the failure to perform an action normally and generally expected, due in response to kindness shown by another person in the past. That response is not merely a private favour requested by the former giver, it is something required by the basic morality of human relationships. 'Gratitude', then, is the very basis of the bonds of mutual obligation that compose 'society', so that 'ingratitude' sets one guilty of it altogether outside the pale of common humanity.

Amiens' song only mentions 'forgetting', but in most of the places where Shakespeare uses 'ingratitude', people are accused of having repaid kindness with cruelty, friendship with enmity, trust with betrayal, love with hatred; that is to say that their behavior shows that they have 'forgotten' the past, not negligently but willfully. They act as if they recognize no duties and obligations, as if the past does not exist, as is suggested in Coriolanus' 'that we have been familiar, Ingrate forgetfulness shall poison' *(Coriolanus V.ii.83)* the present is lived as a denial of the past instead of as a continuation of it and a response to it. The person is saying, 'I exist in and for myself today, alone, I owe nothing to any other.'

Inherent in all this is the dramatic tension of a choice that has to be made: either to turn the back on the person and the past, and return evil for good, or to return good for good. The idea of gratitude suggests duty and continuity in human dealings, mutual obligation. It is for this reason, surely, that modern minds, with their horror of constraints and obligations in relationship, and their infinite desire for individual 'freedom,' do not feel at ease with it.

It is not surprising that the Roman plays often refer to it, with their echoes of the traditional Roman sense of duty and obligation. The morality of Gratitude is part of the underlying structure of *Coriolanus*, where before the election the Third Citizen explains the obligations that are incumbent on them.

If he tell us his noble deeds, we must also tell him our noble acceptance of them. Ingratitude is monstrous, and for the multitude to be ingrateful, were to make a monster of the multitude; of the which we being members, should bring ourselves to be monstrous members. (II.iii.8ff)

Then, when the plot to kill Coriolanus is revealed, Menenius exclaims:

> Nor the good gods forbid
> That our renowned Rome, whose gratitude
> Towards her deserved children is enroll'd
> In Jove's own book, like an unnatural dam
> Should not eat up her own! (III.i.287ff)

http://ccsun7.sogang.ac.kr/~anthony/Ingrate.htm
http://www.pitt.edu/-dash/type0155.html many stories about ingratitude

Mark Twain INGRATITUDE

If you pick up a starving dog and make him prosperous, he will not bite you. This is the principal difference between a dog and a man.

Pudd'n head Wilson

The San Francisco Daily Morning Call, August 24, 1864

INGRATITUDE

George Johnson yesterday had his room-mate, M. Fink, arrested for stealing one hundred and fourteen dollars from him. Johnson says Fink is an old friend of his, and came to him three months ago and said he had no money, could get no work to do, and had no place to sleep; he has previously been tending bar at the Mazurka Saloon. Johnson has shared his bed with him, and paid his washing and board bills from that time until a few weeks ago, when the fellow got a situation of some kind on one of the steamers. He still continued to share Johnson's room, in the Wells Building, corner of Clay and Montgomery streets, however, when in port. Johnson left him in bed yesterday morning, early, and when he returned, he missed his money and his friend—the former from the bureau drawer and the latter from the bed. We consider that this only confirms what we have always said—namely that the heart of man is desperately wicked.

Reader, could you maintain an attitude of gratitude in the face of this betrayal?

One Way Hospitality (Ingratitude)

Once upon a time there were two merchants who wrote letters back and forth to each other. They never met face to face. One lived in Benares and the other lived in a remote border village.

The country merchant sent a large caravan to Benares. It had 500 carts loaded with fruits and vegetable and other products. He told his workers to trade all these goods with the help of the Benares merchant.

When they arrived in the big city they went directly to the merchant. They gave him the gifts they had brought. He was pleased and invited them to stay in his own home. He even gave them money for their living expenses. He treated them with the very best hospitality. He asked about the well-being of the country merchant and gave them gifts to take back to him. Since it is easier for a local person to get a good price, he saw to it that all their goods were fairly traded. They returned home and told their master all that had happened.

Later on, The Benares merchant sent a caravan of 500 carts to the border village. His workers also took gifts to the country merchant. When they arrived, he asked,

"Where do you come from?" they said they came from the Benares merchant, the one who wrote him letters.

Taking the gifts, the country merchant laughed in a very discourteous way and said, "anyone could say they came from the Benares merchant!" Then he sent them away, giving them no place to stay, no gifts, and no help at all.

The caravan workers went downtown to the marketplace and did the best they could trading without local help. They returned to Benares and told their master what had happened.

Before too long, the country merchant sent another caravan of 500 carts to Benares. Again his workers took gifts to the same merchant. When his workers saw them coming, they said to him, "We know just how to provide suitable lodgings, food and expense money for these people."

They took them outside the city walls to a good place to camp for the night. They said they would return to Benares and prepare food and get expense money for them.

Instead they rounded up all their fellow workers and returned to the campsite in the middle of the night. They robbed all 500 carts, including the workers' outer garments. They chased away the bullocks, and removed and carried off the cart wheels.

The villagers were terrified. They ran back home as fast as their legs could carry them.

The city merchant's workers told him all they had done. He said, 'Those who forget gratitude and ignore simple hospitality wind up getting what they deserve. Those who do not appreciate the help they have received soon find that no one will help them anymore."

The moral is: If you don't help others, you can't expect them to help you.

http://www.buddhanet.net/bt_41.htm

Ingratitude

Both soldier and horse went into the wars

They shared much tribulation.

Into cannon fire Horse carried his sire

Each had fierce motivation

With armistice come, went soldier back home

Indulging in pleasures overt.

Brace horse had earned grass, but was fed on chaff,

And weighed down with heavy work

Once more reached all farms the loud call to arms.

Soldier remounted his steed.

"Neigh, nay sire." Horse said, "I've been underfed.

I feel as weak as a weed."

"For you, it's the Foot; but, please Sire, me put

On grass until you return.

To rebuild my strength, so I can, at length

Once more, your gratitude earn."

Deprived of his ride, he turned his carbide

Upon his friend, whom he knew

Still had a dire use despite his abuse.

So turned horse-meat into stew.

Styx's WoW:

The moral is plain from this tale of pain.

Does one desire such an end?

In both war and peace, we musn't ever cease

To take good care of a friend.

http://www.fablesinverse.mcmail.com/Verses/ingratitude.htm

GREAT BIG INGRATITUDE

Andrew Carnegie, the multimillionaire, left $1 million for one of his relatives, who in return cursed Carnegie thoroughly because he had left $365 million to public charities and had cut him off with just one measly million.

Samuel Leibowitz, criminal lawyer and judge, saved 78 men from the electric chair. Not one ever did bother to thank him.

Many years ago, as the story is told, a devout king was disturbed by the ingratitude of his royal court. He prepared a large banquet for them. When the kind and his royal guests were seated, by pre-arrangement, a beggar shuffled into the hall, sat down at the king's table, and gorged himself with food. Without saying a word, he then left the room. The guests were furious and asked permission to seize the tramp and tear him limb from limb for his ingratitude. The king replied, "That beggar has done only once to an earthly king what each of you does three times each day to God. You sit there at the table and eat until you are satisfied. Then you walk away without recognizing God, or expressing one word of thanks to Him."

Ingratitude denotes spiritual immaturity. Infants do not always appreciate what parents do for them. They have short memories. Their concern is not what you did for me yesterday, but what are you doing for me today. The past is meaningless and so is the future. They live for the present. Those who are mature are deeply appreciative of those who labored in the past. They recognize those who labor during the present and provide for those who will be laboring in the future.

Homemade, December, 1984.

Commentary and Devotional

The careless soul receives the Father's gifts as if it were a way that things had of dropping into his hand...yet he is ever complaining, as if someone were accountable for the problems which meet him at every turn. For the good that comes to him, he gives no thanks—who is there to thank? At the disappointments that befall him he grumbles—there must be someone to blame!

George MacDonald

---

http://www.sermonsillustrations.com/a-z/i/ingratitude.htm

Lazy Man's Ingratitude

"I'm ashamed of the way we live," a young wife says to her lazy husband who refuses to find a job. "My father pays our rent. My mother buys all of our food. My sister buys our clothes. My aunt bought us a car. I'm just so ashamed."

The husband rolls over on the couch. "And you damn well should be," he agrees. "Those two worthless brothers of yours ain't never give us a cent!"
The San Francisco Daily Morning Call, August 24, 1864

What Kind of Attitude is Ingratitude?

By F. R. Duplantier

Neglect of the established forms for expressing gratitude may be inadvertent or deliberate. The beneficiary of a gift may neglect to write a thank-you note because he is ignorant of the need for one, because he intends to thank his benefactor in person at some future encounter, or because the press of other obligations encourages him to put it off until he has forgotten about it. Or he may be truly unaware that he has anything to be thankful for, as is the protagonist of the Nabokov novel *The Gift.* In his *Great Expectations,* Charles Dickens tells the story of an ambitious youth who slights his true benefactor by mistakenly attributing his good fortune to someone more neatly fitting his preconceived notions of magnanimity.

Ingratitude may develop naturally from our human tendency to take things for granted. It is easy for us to assume as a matter of course that our parents will feed and clothe and school us, that our friends and relatives will stand by us in time of need, that a job will await us upon graduation, that regular promotions will be ours for the asking, that loving spouses will enter our lives when the time is right, and that loving children will care for us in our dotage. We can easily come to expect these privileges, to look upon them as ours by right, and to conclude that we deserve even more.

The misconstruction of privileges as rights is often an intermediate stage in their transformation into burdens. The bundle of joy that newlyweds long for becomes the due dividend of fertility drugs; this "right," in turn, becomes a daycare-incarcerated drag on the fast-paced careers of ambitious professionals. The petulant child who protests that he "didn't ask to be born" can make a better case for being put upon than the parent who regrets his birth, but both have lost whatever appreciation they may have had for the gift of life, have ceased even to

63

take it for granted, and have adopted a self-defeating, self-sustaining attitude of resentment.

The self-pitier engages in a perverse sort of ledger manipulation, calculating as debits the family and friends, the educational and career opportunities, the affiliations with churches and social groups that should constitute his most valued assets. By undervaluing the gifts and overvaluing the obligations attached to them, he manages to convince himself that not only are they not worth having but that he would be better off without them.

It can be difficult to be grateful to someone who offers what is good for us when what is good for us is not what we want. Often we are grateful for the wrong things, the things that spoil us instead of the things that make us strong. As children we may appreciate the teacher who forgoes homework assignments, the parent who slips us cash without demanding labor in return, and the aunt who plies us with candy; as ignorant, penniless adults with mouths full of cavities, we may take the longer view.

Your Gratitude Inventory

Gratitude is a place, a position in your mind, composed of memories, feelings, deeds and thoughts, all linked together. Your attitude of gratitude comes from the position of this location. When you are living on the surface of gratitude, your perspective is different and as you interpret events from this different perspective, they affect you differently. You go around looking for a gratitude opportunity instead of expecting negative events. You interpret what happens to you as a gift. And then you figure out how you can pay back for the obligation incurred by your acceptance of the gift. We start work on developing this gratitude location in your mind by taking an inventory of the events in your life for which you feel gratitude and start to write them here.

Early life memories of gratitude experiences: _____

_____

_____

_____

Names of people to whom you feel gratitude: _____

_____

_____

_____

Memories of your Ingrate States, taking things-people for granted, living the Ingrate State

_____

_____

_____

Memories of switching from your ingrate state to gratitude.

_____

_____

_____

Events you felt gratitude for and failed to express your gratitude _____

_____

_____

_____

_____

Gratitude for what you have done FOR your family and friends and society

_____

_____

_____

_____

_____

Five events for which you felt gratitude that occurred in the past few days
1. _____
2. _____
3. _____
4. _____
5. _____

Five events which you expressed gratitude in deeds and spread gratitude around
1. _____
2. _____
3. _____
4. _____
5. _____

Good. Now visualize yourself feeling gratitude and returning for what you have been given with a joyous heart. See what you might see, hear the words you might hear and feel the way you will feel as you return for your gratitude in deeds.

Take your gratitude inventory each and every night of your life. Review all of the gratitude moments of the previous day, month, year and monitor your ingratitude so you can switch to, stay in and strengthen your state of gratitude and live in that state as much as possible. Add gratitude to your attitude as way to solve your mental and emotional problems. Button your gratitude button by touching the pad of your left index finger to the pad of your left thumb and connect your memories, feelings, and visions to your gratitude button, that you will use to put yourself into an attitude of gratitude when you need it.

Forming Your Gratitude Button

The word button, as used here, is another word for a classical conditioned response. That is like Pavlov's dogs. The dogs heard a tone sounded at the same time that Pavlov put a few drops of acid on their tongues. The acid made them salivate at the same time that the tone sounded. After a while the tone, when sounded without the acid, caused the animal to salivate and that was called a classical conditioned response. This kind of a response can be used to mentally connect anything to anything else. It is an association formed between two formerly separate events.

Gratitude Healing begins with the word gratitude which itself is a button. Almost all patients look excited when the word is mentioned and all seem to profess that they have a lot of gratitude in their life. This is heart warming to the healer. They all seem to know that Oprah is big on gratitude and the good will they feel towards her spills over into the rush they feel on my saying the word gratitude. I introduce the word in the sessions with my patients during the first visit, by saying, "I feel grateful for your telling me this information". I label several of their behaviors as "That was an expression of gratitude" during the first session and get them started to thinking that they are grateful people in the very first session. That is called a "one word reframe" and I reframe their conduct as showing gratitude or as an expression of the feeling of gratitude whether or not the patient intended it as such. I also serve as a gratitude role model and smile and say, "Thank you, I appreciate your telling me that" and I respond by talking with the patient and putting words back in, to match the words the patient has given me. I talk as much as the patient talks and if the patient doesn't talk a lot, I still talk a lot and put something into the session even though it is hard work and makes me tired and sleepy to do that. I also express my gratitude by listening very carefully to every word the patient says. Intensive listening, with expert understanding and empathy is an expression of gratitude.

I ask every patient to take a food and a gratitude inventory. I ask them to write down all the events of that day for which they feel gratitude. I ask them to write down and describe every instance in which they were in the ingrate state and how and if they worked on their program to get out of the ingrate state into the attitude of gratitude. I also elicit gratitude memories and events in the person's life for which they feel gratitude. These should be made as specific as possible. More specific that just "I feel gratitude for my husband, friends and family." Everyone says that and may or may not mean it. You need specific moments of gratitude for buttoning and you need an overlapped memory composed of visual images, words, feelings, smells and actions of times in the patient's life in which the patient felt gratitude.

A kinesthetic connection is formed by touching the pad of the left index finger to the pad of the left thumb and feeling that touch, while recalling sights, sounds feelings and smells of gratitude experiences in the person's life. Button the gratitude button while recalling gratitude memories. You want to elicit a feeling of heartfelt gratitude and while that feeling occurs, form the gratitude button by touching the pad of the left thumb to the pad on the tip of the left index finger.

I chose the word button for this kinesthetic connection because a button unites two separate pieces of cloth into one united, connected and joined together unit. That is what I refer to as healing. When you break your leg the doctor joins the two broken pieces of bone together. When you have a rupture of the rectus muscles in the abdomen, your doctor sews them together and the join is healing. When you have a broken spirit and feel demoralized, the gratitude button is used to mend the broken parts of your spirit into a fabric of gratitude and that is gratitude healing. Honesty is the only other virtue with nearly the same healing power as gratitude. If you have a dissociation in your mind because you are an habitual liar, then maybe an honesty button would be useful too to mend your fences and join your incongruous parts together. **Healing is the creation of good form through the resolution of incongruity.** It is the matching of what you say with what you do; so your talk matches your walk and your walk matches your talk. You say what you do and do what you say. It is a struggle to create good form where there is poor form in the sense of incongruity or inconsistency. Gratitude can reduce the incongruity of lying, cheating, stealing, envy, greed, egoism, boredom, vice, sloth, carnality, and avariciousness. It can decrease anxiety, depression and gluttony. Sensorimotor feelings of thanks and reciprocating with grateful deeds reduces the incongruity and ill-formedness of mental and physical disorders. That is gratitude healing.

Healing is often achieved by adding an element to your life situation. The added element becomes a director or a coach that points the way, teaches you how to do it, and monitors your performance. Gratitude healing adds gratitude to your mental life and heals you by pulling all your dissociated parts together into a unified connection of gratitude. It is work. It takes work on somebody's part. It requires that you do something different than you have been doing in the past in order to create the good form. It occurs with diverging and converging, with cutting and tying, in separating and joining, in letting go and holding on, in dissociating and associating. Here, we are focusing on restoring your soul and spirit by joining your mind and spirit together with feelings of gratitude.

Weight loss involves a decrease in the incongruity between what you weigh and what you want to weigh or what "they" say you would best weigh for optimum health. You decrease the difference by letting go of some bad choices and by holding on to some good choices in a relationship with a doctor who gives you some suggestions on how to do that.

Serenity joy and happiness involve a resolution of the incongruity between what you expect and what you get. You can get more (or less), you can accept what you have, or you can settle for less. It is all very individual and always based upon the stimulus effects, the situation, your response history, the meaning of the situation and what you intend to do about it.

For some acute diseases healing is achieved by a doctor who cuts something out of your body. You are left with a missing part, which if it is an appendix is not such a big loss. If it is a breast, that is a serious loss and the actual healing requires that you resolve the incongruity caused by your new physical deformity. Think of the several ways that gratitude can heal the broken heart of a person who has had a mastectomy.

1. Button down your gratitude for all the food you love to eat; for the people who fed you; for the people who pay for your food, including yourself; for your life that has been made possible by eating food; and for the food you love to eat. As you think of the most delicious foods you love to eat, that make you feel good, touch your left thumb to your left index finger and connect the feelings of gratitude and delight for the foods you love to eat to your gratitude button. Button, connect, the feelings of gratitude for food to the touch of the left thumb to the left index finger. Good. Way to go. Now open the thumb and index finger and reflect on feeling wonderful in a state of gratitude. Breathe in and out slow and regular, feeling wonderful, feeling grand.

2. You are doing great. Now let your heart and body fill up with a feeling of gratitude from the memory of a gift you were given by someone important in your life. See what you saw, hear what you heard and feel the gratitude you felt receiving that gift and button down your gratitude feelings by closing your gratitude button. Touch your left thumb to your left index finger to button your gratitude button and feel gratitude for the gift you were given. Also feel gratitude for your eyes that see, your legs that walk, your hands that touch. You feel wonderful you feel gratitude and your heart is filled with thanks for the gifts you have been given. Way to go. Feeling gratitude feeling grand. You want to stay in that state of gratitude as long and as often as you

69

can. Good. Now open your touched finger-thumb and relax and meditate on feeling gratitude and thinking how you can repay for the obligation you have incurred by accepting the gift.

3. Meditate on gratitude twice a day and relax take it easy and love yourself. Close you gratitude button and feel gratitude for all of your blessings, all of your family, all of your work, and all of your friends and associates. As you button your gratitude button your heart feels full of gratitude and your stomach feels full of gratitude. You feel full and satisfied and happy.

4. Feel gratitude for looking good and feeling proud of your self and your ability to experience gratitude.

5. Good. Now remember a gratitude memory. Recall a time of gratitude. See what you saw and hear what you heard, feel the gratitude in your heart as you see what you were doing at the moment of gratitude. As you feel gratitude, button your gratitude button and connect that touch with the feeling of gratitude. You will connect the feeling to the touch, so that after you practice this you will be able to put yourself into a state of gratitude by buttoning your gratitude button. Wonderful. See what you saw, hear what you heard, feel that gratitude as you recall what you were doing and imagine a bond is forming between your heart and your gratitude and your gratitude button. You feel an inner peace when you are gratitude. Little things do not bother you. There is a wonderful feeling of closeness. You feel gratitude and it feels wonderful and so do you. Just breathe in and out, slow and regular and feel gratitude where you feel gratitude. Now just slowly open your gratitude button and feel in a mood of gratitude.

    Fine. Now relax and continue in that mode for a while.

6. Good. Now recall someone who has given you something that made you feel fulfilled and happy and grateful. Good. See the face of that person and feel a feeling of gratitude towards that person and, as you do feel that feeling, close your gratitude button, making the gratitude sign and associate that sign with your feelings of gratitude. Feeling wonderful, feeling grand, feeling gratitude. Rehearse the formation of your gratitude button on the memories you wrote into your gratitude inventory from the past and in the present.

7. Great. Now recall a time when you put something back in for what you were given. This may be a situation that requires initiative, where you do something for someone else or for an organization, because your want to show your gratitude and do it to it. As you think of a time when you did

something to show your gratitude, button your gratitude button lightly and get into a position of determination that you will accomplish the goal you have set for yourself to put something back in and to repay your world for what you have received from your world. Think of returning a favor. Think of a time you were giving; a gift you gave and get into this motor expression of gratitude, in which you work hard for someone for the sake of putting something back in. A strange power will come into you, the force will be with you as you determine to show your gratitude, and put your gratitude in action in deeds to match the wonderful feeling of thanks that you have. The most important person at an AA meeting is the one who cleans up, puts the chairs back, and straightens up the mess. He is doing gratitude. Pray in deeds and you will find the true reward for gratitude and living a gratitude lifestyle. When you have the power of gratitude you will be able to overcome any difficulty and do it to the finish line and win. Good. Now release the button, relax and think how wonderful you are and how great you feel when you are returning for what you have been given. Open the button.

8. Wonderful. Now recall a time you acted in a resourceful way. See what you saw, hear what you heard and see what you did when you acted in a resourceful way. When you get into the feeling of acting resourceful, close your gratitude button and feel the force of your resourcefulness uniting into your gratitude sign as you will attach all your resources, your strength and cleverness and personal power into your gratitude button. From now on for the rest of your life you will use all your resources in putting something back in for what you have been given and feel good about yourself. As you contribute to your social interest, you will become more together and attached and feel proud and very grateful. Gratitude is the attitude.

9. Terrific. Feel gratitude for something a special member of your family did for you. See the incident and recall the wonderful experience of feeling gratitude, as you close your gratitude button. Great. Feels good to give thanks in your imagination. You can feel appreciation for what you were given and feel like repaying for the generosity of that special person. Now, release the button, relax, breathe in and out at a slow regular rate.

10. Good. Now get in touch with your personal power and your resources and close your gratitude button tightly as you imagine making a contribution to your family or your job or your favorite charity in order to SHOW YOUR GRATITUDE IN ACTION, IN DEED. You feel wonderful, you feel grand as you use your skills and resources and pay back for what you have been given, by sharing and giving and putting yourself out to show your interest. You do not get paid a lot at first for all you do, but as you will continue to do

it to it, you will receive a payment beyond your present level of comprehension and understanding. You create and get and find yourself, in your doing gratitude and in your showing gratitude and in your giving gratitude. It feels great to earn yourself. Now open the button and relax for a bit.

Visualize an image of what you were doing in a gratitude action. Close the gratitude button and connect the feeling of thanks and appreciation to the gratitude sign. It is this experience of thanks that gives you the personal power to overcome the negativity and turn to your real world and put something back in for what you have been given. This positive force of "putting something back in" for what you feel appreciation, leads you into a social interest and doing for others and for your society. It takes you way beyond the confines of your shame and guilt and enables you to get out of yourself into the limitless spaces where your talents and skills can emerge, evolve and grow.

You were given a nice face and a good body when you were born. You can SHOW YOUR GRATITUDE for this gift of life by taking care of yourself to the best of your ability. You show your gratitude and pay back for what you were given by your mother and father by not smoking, not drinking alcohol, not doing drugs, eating properly, not overeating, dieting if needs be, and by exercising and getting enough sleep and rest. You observe the rules to pay back society for what it has given to you and study hard in school to put something back in return for what your teachers are giving you. It sounds real obvious and real square and real conforming. However, there is no greater treasure than your health, and your education and you show gratitude for your health and your education by taking care of yourself and your environment and studying hard. There is no greater pleasure than inner peace that comes from living in gratitude and returning for the gifts you have been given. Though gratitude is its own reward, it conveys a life of meaning and purpose and love. Would you rather have that or be all screwed up, arrested and in jail?

Good. Go back into your memory and see a picture of yourself receiving a gift for which you feel gratitude in your heart. Some people experienced this in church, some at the dinner table, some in the playing field, some in the office and others in their own places. As you see what you saw and hear what you heard and feel the way you felt when you got the gift, close your gratitude button. It is in this position of gratitude that you will find your true self. That is the surprise gift you get for living a life of gratitude, in the attitude of gratitude. You get yourself back by giving yourself away into the social interest. There is no better deal and no bigger deal in your world. For honest and true, you feel gratitude for finding yourself in giving back for what you have been given. At that point you no longer

72

need games and tricks and falsehoods. You are real. You are for real when you are putting back in for what you have been given and working as hard as you can for that purpose. The benefit also ripples to others in the community and they feel gratitude towards you and you spread your gratitude to them and they spread it around to their family and the consciousness of the world is rising if we can all get into the gratitude life style. That is our best hope for overcoming the differences caused by the envy that is destroying the world. A wind is rising and the river flows as gratitude spreads from me to you and you and you and you.

Monte J. Meldman M.D.

Working on Gratitude

Gratitude is a place, a position in the mind, from which the world is experienced. As events occur, a person living in the gratitude position, with an attitude of gratitude, views and experiences events in the world as gifts regardless of how they do or do not match or mismatch personal expectations, wishes, wants and personal demands. The grateful person feels thanks for the gifts as they are received, and appreciates the gifts by accepting them. Then the person shows gratitude by putting something back in. That something may be a thanks, or a "thank you." It may be returning of the gift in a quid pro quo, or it may be a rather substantial showing of gratitude like spending a year in the Peace Corps, or like Bob Greene writing a great book called DUTY to express his gratitude to his father and General Tibbets.

Constantly working to get on and stay in the position of gratitude is the first way to put something back in for what you have been given. It may not feel real at first. It may be mere words. It may not shake the earth or be a big deal to others, but as you accept the gifts you are given all the time, with an attitude of gratitude, you develop a feeling of inner peace and that special feeling of inner peace feels a lot better than the bone jarring, headache caused by feelings of wrath, revenge, jealousy and envy.

The consequence of living in gratitude is that you feel better, and the blues go away. Self pity yields to peace of mind and happiness comes to you as yet another gift for working on your gratitude position. The process begins with a conscious effort and is learned and internalized by making thousands of gratitude decisions.

A gratitude decision is for sure different than the old ways of revenge, hate and doing it "My Way or the Highway, don't let the door hit you on the way out." A gratitude decision is made because it is in your best interest to make it that way. It is better for you and for your spouse and for your children and friends. It makes everybody feel better.

Can you feel Gratitude when you feel betrayed? Can you feel gratitude or add gratitude to your anger and feel better? Can you feel Gratitude to your wife instead of battering? Can you feel Gratitude as you exercise your Gratitude and Power? Can you anchor your Gratitude State to get over your Negative Mental Attitude? Self Pity? Wrath? Egoism? Jealousy? Bad Attitude? Can you feel Gratitude instead of and while being in control? Can you use Gratitude on your NON-COMPLIANCE, stay in line and follow the instructions and obey the rules? Will Gratitude conquer my evil (in here)? Can your Gratitude overcome your feelings of Injustice? Poor, poor me. Can your Gratitude overcome your thirst for revenge? How will your Gratitude overcome and modify your shame, inferiority, inadequacy, incompetence and weakness? Gratitude is the Attitude. Can you believe it and live that way?

Monte J. Meldman M.D.

Indications for Gratitude Healing

Gratitude programming works by adding gratitude responses to your life. The attitude of gratitude is useful in all four of the following life situations. It is useful when you get what you want, when you get what you don't want, when you don't get what you want and when you don't get what you don't want. You can work it on your memories and in your real life situations by closing the gratitude button, you know how to use, to evoke your attitude of gratitude, and overcome your difficulties in living.

Background Understanding of Gratitude

In her work, "From Envy to Gratitude", the psychoanalyst Melanie Klein says that gratitude arises from the enjoyment and satisfaction experiences the infant has from sucking the breast, being well fed and achieving bliss and contentment. This presupposes a calm mother who understands the infant's needs. Gratitude arises from the satisfaction obtained from what she calls "the good object" and is a beginning of "object relations." Dr. Klein states that "the infant can only experience complete enjoyment if the capacity for love is sufficiently developed" and that it is enjoyment that forms the basis for gratitude. She says that if the undisturbed enjoyment in being fed is experienced frequently, the introjection of the good breast comes about with relative security. Her idea is that the infant forms an internal map of the good breast, and good feeding experience, and she calls this map the "internal object" which is a memory of the breast and the infant feeding experiences. A full gratification at the breast means that the infant feels that he has received from his loved object a unique gift which he wants to keep. This is the basis of gratitude. Gratitude is closely bound with generosity. Inner wealth derives from having assimilated the good object so that the individual becomes able to share its gifts with others. This makes it possible to internalize a more friendly outer world. Thus both forms of gratitude, feeling appreciation and putting something back in, are learned in the first several weeks of life in relation to the mother and the breast feeding.

This ideal situation is complicated by the development of envy of the breast by the infant, which arises naturally because of the constitutional occurrence of envy as a way that the brain functions. Strong envy of the feeding breast interferes with the capacity for complete enjoyment and thus undermines the development of gratitude. Frustrations caused by disrupting breast feeding or interfering with thumb sucking disrupt feelings of gratitude and intensify what Doctor Klein calls the depressive and the paranoid positions.

Primitive envy, along with sadistic biting tendencies, is directed at the breast and the "internal object" and disrupts the loving relationship and trust of the internalized object. Chaucer in "The Parsons Tale" says that envy is the worst sin that is; for all other sins are sins against only one virtue while envy is against all virtue and all goodness. The feeling of having injured and destroyed the primal object impairs the individuals trust in the sincerity of his relations and makes him doubt his capacity for love and goodness. Envy arises naturally out of the function of the difference detector neurons that comprise almost all of the brain. Our learning and cognition is built up of the perception/construction of differences and the perception of differences is accumulated into a map, an internal object, of what we see-hear-feel in the world. Thus envy interferes with the complete enjoyment of the breast and undermines the development of gratitude. Dr. Klein notes that persecutory anxiety and greed (which develops from envy) also disrupt gratitude. Dr. Klein maintains that the child uses the mental mechanism of splitting to preserve the "good object" apart from the "bad object" in order to preserve remnants of the good object, as part of the life instinct, or the separation of love and hate. Jealousy, which is a special case of envy, in which the jealous person envies the relationship two other people have to the exclusion of the jealous person, also interferes with the establishment of a loving internal object.

The formulations advanced by Doctor Klein are somewhat complicated to the uninitiated. Their point as far as gratitude programming is concerned, is that feelings of gratitude are disrupted by envy, jealousy and greed. When doing gratitude programming, the programmer has to be aware of envy, jealousy and greed as feelings that can disrupt the therapy and always work to add gratitude on top of the envy, jealousy, wrath and greed. These feelings interfere with gratitude and love, and have to be dealt with. One needs to stress the benefits of gratitude over the costs of envy, greed, wrath and jealousy. Gratitude does call for a generosity of spirit, a "giving it away in order to keep it" attitude. This may be a very strange way of looking at the world for those whose past relationships have created paranoid anxiety, depression, envy and hate. Gratitude is an alternative to offer people when their old ways have led them to hit bottom and lose everything they have.

Getting What You Want

Gratitude may occur when you get what you want. This is a simple enough motive, derived from the "goal oriented" views of our generation. The object is to set a goal and then accomplish it. There are great rewards for this activity and it is a way to structure time and keep busy. It also is good for making a lot of money. The basic idea behind it is to win, and find surcease in victory. Gratitude

77

should occur when you get what you want, but often getting what you want only sets you up to feel empty and to want more. This is particularly true in the addictions. Alcoholics, drug addicts, obese people, and smokers get what they want almost all of the time and it makes them miserable. There is no satisfaction but only a great high, a recovery of infantile megalomania in which the person feels like God and has a great pleasure for a few moments, only to sink back into the abyss of withdrawal and misery, regrets and poverty. So, getting what you want is only good if what you want is good for you and good for your family and good for our society. Adding gratitude to what you want and seeking out gratitude for what you get is an important step in setting limits on the process. Another problem in getting what you want is that you get so caught up in it that you lose what you already have. How many money successful men have lost their wives and children in the process of becoming a "big man." Gratitude can take you beyond merely getting what you want. If you feel gratitude for what you have been given, you decide to show your gratitude and put something back in for what you have been given. This generosity of spirit is a balance for the insensate greed that is apt to occur in the relentless pursuit of what you want. Generosity implies a sense of obligation that is felt and then fulfilling responsibility in order to pay the obligation is a greater motive than getting what you want. Adding gratitude to the life of those who get what they want is a good step and one that can keep their feet on the ground and lead to genuine happiness instead of bowing to the relentless claims of the ego. A reporter asked Walter Payton how he felt after The Chicago Bears had won the super bowl. He looked bewildered and said, "I feel empty. Very empty". When you get what you want, you lose what you want because you already have it, so you cannot want it any more. It is very hard (impossible) to want what you already have.

Gratitude is the core of recovering from addictions. The great "I AM" comes into treatment wrecked and bent out of shape from getting what he/she wants. The first step is to work on the denial of the sickness that has occurred from getting what I want. The next step is to join a treatment process. The next step is to give up the object of addiction, to quit drinking and to quit drugging and to quit eating sweets and to give up a love object for the sake of staying alive. Gratitude is installed at this point. The person learns to feel grateful for letting go of a love object for the sake of staying alive. Then gratitude is the measure of health and as long as the person is living in the state of gratitude, the sickness is usually in check.

Gratitude demands that you put back in for the obligation you have incurred in getting what you want. You have to feel gratitude when you get what you want or the victory is ill-formed, and it will go on and on until it kills you.

Imagine getting what you want. Say thank you to the people who helped you get it. Do thank you for the society that helped you get it. Put something back in for what you have been given. Those Hollywood stars who find sudden riches without gratitude get into drugs, divorce and all kinds of ill formed behavior. Paul Newman puts back in for what he has been given and is a happy and a wise man. And yes, he has had more trouble than you have had in your life. Try losing your son for starters. Gratitude balances success. Without gratitude, success is ill-formed. Freud's most famous and best title is "Some Character Types Wrecked By Success". He knew how bad success can unbalance and ruin your life.

Imagine being successful. See your victory. Feel wonderful and victorious and successful. Good. Now close you gratitude button and feel gratitude for your success and imagine you will put something back in, return a whole bunch, for what you have been given by others and society. Put something back in for the food you have been given by eating well, following my plan, going on a diet and exercising or getting the food you want will make you fat and sick. Being a great big work success can cost you your wife and children. Some success. Being a great big rich man can turn you into a number one prize goof unless you balance it off with gratitude.

Not Getting What You Want

Adding gratitude for not getting what you want is the next step in the recovery from addiction. This is exactly not what people who are goal directed are looking for. If you love sweets and sugar, it is strange to work on feeling gratitude for not getting what you love. But this is exactly what you need to do in order to get over the bad effects of getting all the sugar and candy you want. It is not good to get what you want when what you want is ruining your figure and your teeth and your face and making you have regrets and feel lousy. Gratitude will take the place of the lost love object. Some day you will relate that this is the best decision you ever made in your life. But you have to remember your gratitude and keep it up every day. I feel grateful that I do not smoke tobacco any longer and that it took a terrible pain in the leg and a blood clot to get me to stop smoking. I could not do it on my own or with the help of therapy. I was given the gift of a blood clot in the femoral artery and every time I smoked after that it hurt my leg like mad. The pain in the leg that got worse when I smoked made me give it up and so I did not get the stroke that was awaiting me as the reward for all of my smoking. I feel grateful that I have a blood clot in my leg, even though it impairs my motility, and is a pain. It is my gift for which I feel gratitude and I will not have it revised (only to die in surgery like Edmund Muskie!)

The love that gets away from you and goes with another should be a source for gratitude. Feel gratitude when you are dumped! It was not right. It was not meant to be. She is gone. Feel gratitude instead of self pity. You were spared a lot of anguish. Poor you. Feel gratitude and put something back into your society for the extra time you no longer have to waste chasing her. You're only a fool if you do not recognize unrequited love and getting dumped as a gratitude opportunity. After reading this paragraph, a friend of a patient went to sleep for twelve hours for the first good sleep she had had since she was dumped by a man she loved who did not love her. What did she lose? A life of misery at best. Gratitude for blessings received.

It is good to not get what you want when what you want is not good for you, your family and your country. Feel gratitude for what you missed: heartache, misery, pain. Poor baby you don't get what you want, when you should not get what you want. It is good not to get the food you want, for then you are losing weight. It is good not to lose all the weight you want to lose in two weeks for you might die if you lost all the weight you want to lose as quickly as you want to lose it. Feel gratitude for disappointment and frustration. Those are gratitude opportunities and do not pass them up.

Getting What You Don't Want

There are events in life that are too much to bear. I do not wish to minimize the pain and suffering that we go through in this veil of tears. Our fondest expectations are blown away. Our greatest hopes are wrecked. How can you feel when your child dies suddenly of meningitis? How can you go on living when a drunk smashes into your car and your wife dies in your arms? Denial. Anger. Grief. Despair. Detachment. Madness. Suicide. Those are the biological givens that our tears and convulsive crying work on. Yet sometime it might be possible to feel gratitude for what you had and what you were given. I can't imagine feeling grateful for a cancer of the breast or a heart attack. That would not make any sense. But just because it does not make any sense does not disqualify it from being a valid response to tragedy. Who knows how it will turn out if you feel grateful instead of enraged? Who knows if gratitude does not have a better outcome than despair? Feeling gratitude for what you have been given is one possible spiritual position and it is only crazy to those who do not know the power of gratitude. Adding gratitude to your life can make the worst of situations bearable, so why not work on it when in your darkest moments? Gratitude works. Giving thanks for what you have is not a bad idea in good times and bad. Maybe it is another valid way to find meaning and make sense out of this thing we call living. It is if it works to help you feel better and get over your grief, terror and depression.

Not Getting What You Don't Want

It is not difficult to see how you might feel gratitude for not getting what you don't want. It is wonderful to pass an exam you thought you flunked. Feel gratitude in your heart for that one. It is a time for gratitude when the doctor tells you the lump in your breast is not cancer but merely a liquid containing cyst. It is great to find out you do not need a prostatectomy. It is wonderful to find out you were not fired. Rejoice. Feel wonderful. Feel gratitude and thanks in your heart. Take someone out for a celebration and share your joy with them. You will find that you have more people to go out with you and share your joy if you have lived a life of gratitude and given thanks for what you have been given and for what you were not given. Gratitude makes you more happy and that makes others more happy and they like to be with you.

Good. Now button your gratitude button and remember that time when you did not get what you did not want and feel happy and grateful for that. Wow, it's wonderful, isn't it? You complained about the dark until you heard the cane of a blind man. Feel gratitude you are not blind, crippled, broke and ruined. It is terrible to lose your job and not have any money. Feel gratitude you can see and hear.

Losing What You Have

It is real hard to feel grateful when you lose someone that you have loved and cared for. It is sad. It is hideous. It is unfair. It is wrong. It is real bad. It is horrible to watch helplessly and see them suffer. It is real bad to lose your job and to run out of money. It is real bad to get sued when you do not feel guilty and to get punished when it is not fair. Injustice is hard to swallow. The usual responses are rage, getting even, lashing back and hurting, protest and blaming. That is as it should be. But how can you recover from such disasters after they have ruined your life? I don't really know. Each of us finds our own path. Someone helps us out. We find stability in exercise or wandering around lost or going mad or finding a good therapist. One of the constants in this ever-changing world is a feeling of gratitude for what is and putting something back in for what you have been given. It may be dumb. It may be too much to ask. Anchor your life in gratitude and see how that works out, see how that lets you feel. Close your gratitude button and while making the gratitude sign, recall a time you felt gratitude and it felt good. You felt satisfied and whole and complete and all together. Good. Work on your attitude of gratitude and use it as you will to solve some of the problems that occur in this world of injustices. Life is not fair. You can even feel gratitude for that, and get over collecting injustices and get on with your happiness.

Ingratitude

We care for the ravages of ingratitude with gratitude healing. This begins when the person cannot take the pain and discomfort of the consequences of ingratitude. The patient "hits bottom" when the pains are too much to bear; when the fat protrudes all over and the pants don't fit even though they have been stretched a lot; when the smoking causes emphysema and inability to breathe; when the batterer gets put in jail; when the alcoholic vomits pure blood; when the marriage dissolves in violence; when the crook is in the jail. We listen carefully to the denial and the excuses and the blames and the injustices and the rationalizations. Then we reframe the disease as a consequence of ingratitude and start to teach the person about gratitude and how it can relieve those sadistic feelings and create an inner peace that is worthwhile. We get the person hooked up with other grateful people who provide a "holding environment" and the person emerges into a state of gratitude which provides a calm in the storm. Self pity gives way to gratitude, as does denial and projection and blaming. We encourage the person to spread gratitude around and look for gratitude experiences in life and then as the treatment works and the person" spirits lift up, a recovery is in process and the results of that are amazing to see.

Negative Mental Attitude

Negativity is its own curse. You expect negative, you get negative and you feel relief and say, "Aha, I was right." You look forward in dread and predict that bad things will happen. Somehow that gives you a magical control and you feel that you control bad things by expecting them. If you expect them, they won't happen. If they don't happen, the best you can feel is a sense of relief. If they do happen, you can feel you expected it and that makes you not too upset. You can put a negative spin on everything and everyone. It makes you feel superior to hear the ten o'clock news and hear the terrible things that happen to others. This is a lousy world and the news verifies that because the news is all negative. The TV news has become a universal mental illness characterized by negativity. Negativity usually adapts to what isn't. It is a prediction of a doom that has not occurred. It is a reaction to something that isn't. It derives its power as a defense against loss and death. They are our real and constant companions in life. You choose if you prefer, to adapt to life and feel gratitude, or adapt to death and loss and go negative. Negativity is the path to pain and failure.

Gratitude Healing Techniques

Continue working on your gratitude inventory. Remember the PAIN/consequences of ingratitude and do not act out your ingratitude.

Take Your Inventory Of Your Ingrate States and Your Gratitude Moments

Take your Gratitude Inventory of your past life. Take your Ingrate State Inventory. Learn how you feel and act when in your ingrate state. Learn how you feel gratitude. Write down your gratitude moments and your ingrate states of today each night so that you can see/hear/feel them clearly and then proceed to learn how to move yourself from your ingrate state into gratitude. Record these triumphs in your gratitude inventory each night. Keep gratitude where it belongs, in the front of your mind. Sleeping with gratitude is a good way to sleep.

Put A Gratitude Spin On The Gifts Of Your Life

Interpret the people and events that occur in your life as gifts for which you feel gratitude. Put the gratitude spin on all the events of your life. Each event is a gift. You intend to pay back for the gift you have been given. Be careful not to seek revenge. Twist revenge into gratitude and kill them with kindness.

This takes some doing for the uninitiated. The ingrate states of anger, revenge, injustice collecting, self pity, envy, jealousy, "poor me", that's not fair, fear, worry, abusing others, self abuse and addiction to alcohol, drugs, nicotine, marijuana, heroin, food and coffee are too real to be dismissed by a first attempt at gratitude spinning. The claims of "The Great I Am" and the egotistical attempts to be superior and inferior at the same time have been done so often for so long that they seem like the only reality. It takes a lot of training and doing to learn to spin or interpret events into the position of gratitude. It takes more than a little imagination and creativity to feel grateful for losing your job and not having any money. Maybe it isn't a good idea to always try to fit every event in your world into the gratitude position. But barring life threatening situations, the best way out of the ingrate state is to interpret as much as you can into the gratitude position. Maybe the reason you lost your job and don't have any money is because you spent your life in an ingrate state and your boss couldn't stand you any more so he got rid of you. Possible? An eye for an eye and a tooth for a tooth will soon leave you blind and toothless. Is that what you want?

83

Detect And Correct Living In The Ingrate State.

We get into The Ingrate State too easily and it is hard to detect when you are acting out of the ingrate state unless you constantly monitor your attitude and know what to look for. Denial and projection are the mental mechanisms of the Ingrate State. We deny that we are the problem and we project all of the trouble onto the world and other people around us. Blaming others, fate, life situations, luck and past history are the hallmarks of the ingrate state. There are many types of Ingrate States but for our purposes here we can mention Ingrate Type I and Ingrate Type II. Ingrate State Type I is grandiose and punishes others for real, imagined and threatened transgressions. Ingrate State Type I always has an answer in his mouth, blames others, lies, cheats, steals, slips and slides and hides from responsibility. Ingrate Type I is mean, brutal, inflicts pain on others and batters and abuses physically and mentally. This state is often seen in alcoholics and drug addicts who get nailed into addiction by their refusal to accept and abide by the limits that civilized people accept and respect. Ingratitude does not give any credit to others. The Ingrate imagines he is always the top of the heap. Ingrate Type I has shallow feelings and little loyalty. Ingrate Type I is an aggressor.

The Ingrate State Type II feels inferior and ashamed and blames the self, but still blames, makes excuses, lies, cheats, steals, and slips and slides out of responsibility, or, accepts more responsibility than possible and is always complaining about how others do not do their share. Ingrate Type II has negativity all through the thought processes. Fear begets fear. Depression is part of self-pity. Fear and depression rotate side by each. Negative thinking, negative evaluations, negative interpretations if strong enough, lead to a paranoid transformation, which blames "them" for all of the negative things that happen to Ingrate Type II. Ingrate Type II is a victim.

You know you are in your Ingrate State I when you are aggravated, turbulent and want to hurt someone. You are mad as hell and want to argue and inflict pain verbally or physically on someone clearly weaker than yourself. You are in an Ingrate State II if you are afraid and depressed and full of self-pity. You are in an Ingrate State if you want revenge and you want to hurt someone in order to get justice and to get even. You are in an Ingrate State when you feel sorry a lot and fight against the river and are disagreeable and always have to have your own way.

Your ingratitude is showing when you don't feel like doing a job to the best of your ability.

Gratitude is both a feeling and a doing. The motor part of gratitude is "putting something back in for what you have been given." You need to pay back in a positive sense for everything society has given you and for what your parents and teachers did for you and for what you owe America and God. Gratitude defines an obligation or is defined by obligation. It is a debt you owe and your life becomes what you are in the process of paying back for what you have been given. Ingrate Type III is a dead beat who blows off his debts and denies what others have done for him and takes it all for granted.

ADD GRATITUDE TO YOUR INGRATE STATE TO TRANSFORM INTO GRATITUDE

You need to close your gratitude buttons when you slip into an Ingrate State in order to add gratitude to your Ingrate State. Healing occurs in this homospatial fusion of gratitude with the feelings, ideas, sights and sounds of The Ingrate State. Healing occurs through addition of ideas, feelings and thoughts that formerly were incongruous with gratitude. When you feel self-pity, fuse that feeling with gratitude in the same time/place by adding your memories and feelings of gratitude to your feelings of self pity. See where this incongruous fusion will take you. See if gratitude can heal the splits in your soul and the splits in your mind, delivering you into a new state composed of the previous ingrate state plus gratitude.

For example, recall a time when you felt angry and wanted to lash out and punish someone or get back at them in revenge. See what you saw, hear what you heard and feel the feeling of anger wrath and revenge. You remember feeling really mad and step into that picture now and feel that feeling. When you get good and mad, or when you can recall the angry scene, see a visual image of that experience in which you were mad, good and irritated. O.K. now button your gratitude button and see the face of a person to whom you feel gratitude. Work on combining the anger with the gratitude experience and see what happens. Does adding gratitude change the picture of wrath? If not, do it again. Add more gratitude logs to the fire of your anger until you can get it to change, and you create a new state composed of anger and gratitude, wrapped up together into a creative fusion. Good that is the idea. Work on your feelings by adding gratitude and see if you can create a new state that is more adaptive and has a better outcome for you than getting mad.

85

Gratitude Visualizations

See what you will see and hear what you have heard and feel the way that you have felt when you were grateful for a gift that was given to you. Do this several times a day. Then, see yourself paying back for what you have been given and fulfilling the obligation you have to pay back for what you have been given. Not to do an act is as much of an act as to perform an act. Therefore, one thing you can do in order to pay back for all the food you have been given is to eat in gratitude and to make good choices in the foods you choose.

You can publish your gratitude in the local newspaper and in the Internet. Then pay back for that gift.

Bring your gratitude to group and discuss it. The single hardest event in the world is to change your mind and to interpret events in your life into the gratitude framework, as a gift, and desire to put back in for what you have been given. Do not dwell on the pity pot. Get into the attitude of gratitude and live and love it. Gratitude spreads and spreads from me to you and you and you and you.

We mentioned the possibility that you can feel gratitude when you get what you don't expect or don't want. That is one time in which you can button your gratitude button and add gratitude to an unpleasant situation in a creative fusion. This is gratitude healing and it consists of the homospatial connection of the feeling of gratitude with the feelings associated with getting what you don't want. This is a creative process and the outcome is not known. You intend to change your current state of mind by adding gratitude to your current state of mind and produce a new and different state of mind. This is how gratitude can heal your pain and reduce the splits in your soul and the splits that occur between yourself and others and it can lead to forgiveness of yourself for your errors.

Healing Fear and Anxiety

Some fears are good to have. They protect you from harm. Our fear mechanism has been built in over centuries and warns us when we are in trouble, or about to get hurt. It certainly is OK to be afraid and to admit that and to listen to it. Lack of fear can get you into a heap of trouble. But some fears are not adaptive and not helpful. They are false alarms and say that a situation is dangerous when it is not dangerous. These fears are called anxiety and result from negative thinking and negative expectations and false alarming, saying we are about to get hurt when we are not. These fears are paralyzing and put us in a box that gets smaller and smaller as the years go on. We add gratitude to these anxieties in order to get over the anxiety and turn this feeling into a resource, that we can use in other areas of our life. Recall a time when you felt anxious. Maybe stage fright? Maybe a time you felt you would fail a test and were going to get scolded. See what you saw and hear the words in your head and feel the way you felt when you were anxious and filled with dread when it was excessive and not appropriate. Good. When you reactivate that anxiety memory, close the gratitude button and overlay the anxiety with gratitude. This is a stretch. Twist the anxiety feelings into a gratitude situation. Like feel gratitude that all the people are looking at you and you return for what you have been given by giving them a great performance. They applaud to show their gratitude. You do your best and accept the applause and feel wonderful as you will overlay your anxiety with gratitude. The cage of fear opens up and you can come out into the sun and feel wonderful. See. Gratitude works to overcome fear and it is a rational thing to do. Get professional help when this is needed.

Shame and Inferiority Feelings

Think about a part of your body of which you feel ashamed. Maybe you are short. Maybe you are too fat in the thighs. Maybe you are dumb. Maybe you are poor. Maybe you didn't go to college. Maybe you didn't go to the right college etc. etc. etc. There is absolutely no end to the things you can feel ashamed about. Shame is part of envy, for if the other person has something so great, then it follows that what you have is inferior and a shame on you. Find a flaw on your body and focus your shame on that part. Good. Now imagine you feel gratitude for the part of yourself that you are ashamed of. Add gratitude to the shame you feel about your fat belly. As you feel that hot feeling of shame, close your gratitude button and then let the gratitude mix with the shame and see what happens. Feel gratitude for your shame for it has led you to try to be better than others to overcompensate for your shame.

Again, get in touch with your shame feelings, feel small inadequate and inferior, and then button your gratitude button to join and combine a feeling of gratitude with that feeling of shame. Shame-gratitude is a different state and use this creative fusion, created by the mingling of two feeling states, to change your shame and to lead your talents into putting something back into society for what you have been given. This needs a lot of work, for outside of self-doubt, there is no more common mental negative than shame and inferiority feelings.

Again, in your imagination, compare yourself to someone else and feel ashamed and inferior about yourself. Then close the gratitude button and feel gratitude. See what happens in that mix of shame and gratitude. You can spring out of the shame trap by giving and generosity to others. Create your own solution, letting gratitude be your guide.

Stage Fright

Imagine you are in front of a group of people and about to give a speech and you feel afraid. Now button your gratitude button and feel gratitude to all the people who are paying attention to what you have to say. Give a great speech to pay them back for their attention and feel gratitude to the audience for their applause. You will feel wonderful. Focus on gratitude and returning for what you have been given rather than on what you might lack.

Grandiosity and Wrath

Imagine that you are up on your high horse. You feel superior to the other. You criticize them. You look down your nose at them. You feel superior to them. You are mad at them and you hurt their feelings by saying bad things to them. Maybe you even batter her, and shove her around and choke her throat. As you remember a time you felt real angry, stop for a moment and feel gratitude for what you have and for what has been done for you. You do not feel hate when you are in gratitude. You feel peace of mind and feel good about yourself. Close your gratitude button, touch your left thumb to your left index finger and put yourself into a state of gratitude so you will not act out on your temper and that thirst for revenge. Instead let your gratitude come to the top and pay back in love for what you have been given and feel happiness and wonderful as you escape from the trap of hate and grandiosity. Work on gratitude, not hate. Return love and let go of power and control. If you are a jealous freak with feelings of inferiority and you imagine you wife is unfaithful, close your gratitude button on that and feel gratitude that she is unfaithful (in your imagination or for real) and that is a great feeling. It will arouse you sexually and you will perform better than him. Do it to it in sex. Not in hitting.

Rejection and Criticism

Maybe you have rabbit ears and cower before people who criticize and put you down. If so, imagine a situation in which you felt hurt and rejected by critics and get in touch with that feeling of being hurt and criticized. Fine. Now recall a gratitude memory from your inventory of gratitude memories and put yourself into a state of gratitude.. Let the gratitude cover over those feelings of rejection and worthlessness. You feel grateful for the opportunity to improve yourself. Feel gratitude in your heart and figure out how to combine the gratitude with all your other feelings so that you experience the thankfulness and wonder of gratitude.

Feeling Depressed and Down

We feel sad and grieve under many circumstances but often when we have experienced the loss of a loved one. Crying and sadness is a normal part of living and under certain circumstances is all we can do about the loss of a loved one. Depression is different than grief and bereavement. It is more like a physical disease sometimes for which we need a medication. Sadness and self-pity and feeling sorry for yourself are perhaps forms of physical depression but also may contain elements of ingratitude. We get into self pity as a routine for feeling sorry for ourselves for what isn't, for what we do not have. That type of depression is the focus of gratitude healing. Recall a time when you got into your "poor me" status. You felt others had more than you did and that "it isn't fair" that they have it so good and you do not. Recall a memory of ingratitude in which you felt depressed that you didn't get your way and felt deprived of something you wanted. As you get into that memory, close your gratitude button and add gratitude to your feelings to change them. Combine that "poor me" state with your state of gratitude and let gratitude take you over so you feel glad about what you do not have! Yes, even jealousy can give way to gratitude. Let the creative part of your mind give the part of you that feels sad and depressed several new alternative gratitude behaviors that to your surprise and delight will attach themselves to your self-pity and sadness and let you get out of the self-pity box into a new and better level of functioning, feeling wonderful, feeling grand, feeling gratitude.

Gratitude for Suffering

We often seek to avoid and escape suffering. That just makes good sense. Or does it? You have to suffer greatly to become a great athlete. Training rituals are incredibly punitive. So are coaches. You have to suffer greatly to get through medical school and become a doctor and then you have to suffer a lot to become a good doctor and put up with all the rules that are dumped on your head. You have to pay the cost of the effort and the opportunity cost of everything you have to give up in order to focus on what you want to achieve. When you are on a diet to lose weight you have to suffer to give up the foods you like to eat and to feel hungry perhaps for the first time in years. You will feel hungry and feel gratitude for hunger and suffering because that means you are losing weight. In AA you will feel gratitude for all the suffering you experienced in your life as a drunk because that suffering is what led you to AA and you are a grateful alcoholic because your drunkenness led you into the program and the salvation of your spirit in the program. Not bad.

It is too trite to say "No pain, No gain." How can you suffer unless you hope that the end result will lead to gratitude. So, gratitude is often not an inappropriate response for your suffering. If you were dead you would not be suffering. Job (pronounced Jobe; there is a book about him and his suffering in the bible. Read it.) found his suffering was wonderful in that it proved he was connected with God. What more can a person ask for than that? Jesus suffered for your sins in the Christian way of thinking. If you believe in Him, you will get eternal after-life in Heaven. Jesus suffering is a metaphor for the fact that you have to suffer to achieve a goal. To be like Jesus is to suffer and be betrayed by your friends. That is why you can feel gratitude when your friends betray you...and they most certainly will. Why should you be any different than me and everyone else? When you are betrayed, feel gratitude that you are rid of the scum and move on into a better life.

Attitude of Gratitude

Posted by Barbs on July 19, 1997 at 15:22:30:

Today I can work on my attitude. When I nurture an "Attitude of Gratitude" it is amazing how people, places and things around me improve. I can start it in the morning by doing something good for myself—a walk, even though it may follow the same path daily, there are many things along the way that constantly change (as I do when working my program) clouds, flowers, people etc. I just need to remember to keep my eyes, ears and mind open. That is often the time when my Higher Power communicates with me.

An "Attitude of Gratitude" helps me to focus on the positives in my life. Today I do have a Higher Power who will guide me through the day if I allow Him. When I do allow Him to guide me, my day goes much better. I need to practice keeping the lines of communication open as I am often amazed by those lines—it may be someone called me and the words of wisdom exiting from my mouth in no way originated in my thoughts, or the other people let into my world to teach me a lesson so desperately needed but not requested.

As Today's Reminder from "One Day at a Time" says on Jan. 6, "When things look blackest, it is within my power to brighten them with the light of understanding and gratitude. I realize how much depends on my point of view; my own wrong habits of thinking and acting must be corrected and only I can do that."

I am grateful today for the All-Anon program which has taught me how to have an "Attitude of Gratitude."

Love and peace,
Barbs Friends of Alanon

Expressing the Gifts of Gratitude

By Rev. Leroy Zemke

"Two roads diverged in a wood, and I took the one less traveled by, and that has made all the difference." Robert Frost

"The real miracle is not to walk either on water or in thin air, but to walk on Earth," Nhat Hanh

All around us are gifts, gifts that emerge in tender moments, fragile places, silent spaces awaiting their ultimate disposition within the human heart. What is required of the givers and the receivers is an openness to the fullness of life that reaches far beyond the gift itself. Here we are—momentarily lifted far beyond our ordinary selves into the world of the incredible, the beautiful, the bountiful and radiant, the hopeful and the truly transcendent.

Let me share a story that may further illustrate this premise far more eloquently than the language in which it will be clothed, more poetically than cascading ribbons or iridescent light and shadow in the tumbling waters of a waterfall. Only the names have been changed.

Beth, a tired, frightened young mother clutched her only child closely to her bosom seeking to comfort and calm her little one's distress and soothe her fears. Then she put her back in her bed, only to pick her up again in a few minutes and repeat the same efforts over and over again. This marked the second night that her three year old Rebeccah alternately awakened, fitfully cried, and fell back to sleep. Her hot face and fevered body never cooled and her breathing had become labored and short.

"Oh, God," Beth cried out, "Help me! Help me! Help me! Help me to help Rebeccah!" Beth's husband, Bob, had to stay one more day in California to finalize the details of a year long contract negotiation, a business deal he had hoped and dreamed would come together. And now it was happening! Finally happening. It would bring badly needed income after a year of severe struggles and hardships, cruel disappointments and rejection after rejection! But Bob wasn't there...and she needed him desperately. Beth turned her attention to the feverish child again and sobbed in her anguish. Alone. Frightened. Finally Beth decided that she would dress, bundle Rebeccah up in blankets, and they would drive across the snow-crusted countryside to the little hospital nearly thirty miles away. It was midwinter and bitterly cold. The time was nearly five o'clock in the morning. She worried, what if the car wouldn't start? What if they got on their way and the car stalled, as it tended to do in cold weather? These and nameless fears possessed her as she dressed. She tried to distract herself momentarily by attempting to remember the lyrics of an old hymn.

"Rrrinng! Ring...ring." Beth was startled back to her senses. The doorbell? Surely she had imagined the doorbell's rrinngg!" The tone was deliberate and persistent. "Oh, God," Beth thought, "What do I do now? Oh, God, I'm alone!"

WHY did Bob have to stay one more day? Who could be ringing the doorbell at this hour? Oh, God, I'm frightened!"

Beth started toward the door and then stopped. The ringing continued. Unexpectedly, she stopped feeling frightened and confused. Something inside her being, deep inside her very soul, called to her and gently urged her, "Go to the door." Beth followed the directive. At the door, she paused again before opening it. She was responding mechanically, as if she were in a dream, and none of what she was experiencing was real. Then she opened the door. There in the darkness of the early morning stood a young woman dressed very much like herself, who spoke to her quickly.

"Do you have a young daughter who is ill?" Beth was so startled, she could only gasp and answer, "Yes, yes...she's very feverish and her breathing is difficult..." Her voice trailed off. The woman spoke reassuringly and asked if she might enter and visit with the child. "Yes, please come in," murmured Beth.

Beth led the unknown visitor to the child's room. The young woman leaned over and gently stroked the fitful Rebeccah's head, picked up her hand, and then paused and kissed her on the forehead. With a calming demeanor of peaceful serenity, she gradually turned to Beth and said, "Rebeccah will be fine by noon today and she will gain strength every day." The mysterious stranger than announced that she must leave and slowly went back to the door.

Somewhat bewildered and yet inexplicably reassured, Beth accompanied her and tried to thank her. The young woman held up her hand and said, "Remember your prayer...'God, help me'...I have been sent to help you." She smiled at Beth, with a smile that seemed to convey a world of care and trust...looked back in Rebeccah's direction again. Almost effortlessly, she quietly opened the door and stepped outside, gently closing the door behind her and was gone. By noon Rebeccah's fever was indeed gone and her breathing was keep and easy. And she improved each day thereafter as the young woman had promised.

In telling the story, Beth now feels that they were visited by an angel, an angel who brought the profound gift of healing to Rebeccah. Nothing and on one will ever convince Beth otherwise. There are many gifts in this story. Certainly the gift of healing, however it occurred, is most remarkable in and of itself and all that it offers and implies. It is many layered.

But what of Beth's willingness to trust her deeper impulse or intuition to open the door? Unquestionably, her rational self said "no." Yet she responded to something beyond her personal self and her fear based emotional dilemma.

And what of the gift that in finally asking God to help her. Is this not a major gift unto itself? We often seek for gifts that life might offer us, but fail to recognize the gifts because of the covering that enwraps them (the circumstances).

The Expressing of Gratitude then, is really about learning how to listen; now to be open to inner guidance when it is needed and how to receive what is offered. Yes, gratitude is a thankful attitude, a thankful heart, a feeling which is held and offered from the depths of our innermost spirit.

It is an approach to our larger nature through the various doorways of life that gently call us to remember that God is in charge, indeed, of our lives, far more than we may see or know or believe.

"Because thou hast made the Lord, which is my refuge, even the most High, they habitation; therefore shall no evil befall thee, neither shall any plague come nigh unto thy dwelling. For he shall give his angels charge over thee, to keep thee in all thy ways. They shall bear thee up in their hands, lest thou dash thy foot against a stone." Psalm 91:9-12

GRATITUDE TO THE UNKNOWN INSTRUCTORS

By William Butler Yeats

What they undertook to do

They brought to pass;

All things hang like a drop of dew

Upon a blade of grass.

Gratitude and Weight Loss

When you feel grateful for the body and face you have been given by your genes and all the work your mother and father did for you, you "put something back in" by taking good care of yourself. Show your gratitude for what you have been given by working out, eating properly, taking care of your teeth, practicing good health habits. If you take your body for granted and do not take good care of yourself with good eating habits, you are living in an ingrate state, and will sooner or later come to regrets. You want to avoid regrets, if you feel gratitude for what you are and what you have been given.

Gratitude gives you a different perspective on life, and enables you to think thoughts that are different than the thoughts you have in the ingrate state. When you want to gain a different perspective on food and change your eating habits, you can work on feeling gratitude for feeling hungry. You can work on adding feelings of gratitude to the emptiness you feel when you have not eaten for a while. You can meditate on gratitude instead of eating and meditate on foods you need to eat in order to feel gratitude about your weight and your shape. You also learn to feel gratitude to yourself as you turn down food that is not in your eating plan.

Members of AA often say that they are grateful alcoholics. They mean that they are happy they are alcoholics because that enabled them to join AA and they are grateful for the wonders that the fellowship has worked in their lives. Perhaps you will some day feel gratitude for the wonders that the Gratitude Therapy works in your life. I hope so.

Good. Now imagine that you are in a place at a time in which you feel hungry. Perhaps you can even feel that hunger now. Good. Now reflect on one of the memories from your gratitude inventory. As you will add gratitude to your hunger, you realize that accepting your hunger and feeling gratitude for it will lead you in the direction of losing the weight you want to lose and you will feel gratitude for the weight you lose and having a nice figure.

Great. Now think about walking on past a candy display of your very favorite sweets and you decide not to get any, to turn it down, and walk on by and feel gratitude for your ability to turn down sweets and carbohydrates. As you feel that feeling of gratitude, you will feel that inner peace that comes with gratitude and that will reinforce your decision to turn down sweets and you will go for that feeling of inner peace that comes from feeling gratitude for what you have been given.

Now I ask you to focus your gratitude on the part of your mind that says "No" or "Cut it out" or "Just Don't" when you are confronted with temptation to eat something that is not in your eating program. Yes, instead of rebelling against your conscience, I would ask you to show your gratitude by complying with the dictates of your conscience and feel gratitude to your conscience for its intention to protect you and to enable you to stay healthy and avoid the ravages of obesity.

Good. Imagine the TV show is over and you are going to bed and you feel like going into the refrigerator or the pantry and eating a little bit before going to bed. As you move towards the kitchen and the food you know is there, listen to the voice saying "Skip it. Pass it up. You don't need it. You had enough to eat today." Fire the gratitude anchor, clench your fist and let a feeling of gratitude be directed at your conscience. Listen to what your conscience tells you and go along with the program. Pass it up and go on up to bed and let it go. You will feel gratitude for your ability to control yourself and you empower your conscience and let your conscience control your actions; let your conscience be your guide. You feel wonderful. You feel grand. You feel good about yourself. YOU FEEL GRATEFUL TO YOUR CONSCIENCE. You love your conscience and all the good things it intends to do for you. Sleep tight with a clear conscience and an empty stomach for which you feel gratitude.

Imagine you come to the office and you "only" lose four pounds in two weeks. You curse and gnash your teeth in disappointment. You expected to lose so much more weight. You declare it is not fair to "only" lose four pounds because you worked so hard and barely ate a lettuce leaf all two weeks. Good. You feel angry, frustrated and disappointed. Now close your gratitude button and add gratitude to your feelings so maybe you can feel gratitude for losing the four pounds. Feel gratitude you did not gain six pounds and you are looking better and feeling good.

Gratitude In Divine Healing

The receptivity of the patients can be enhanced by silently or verbally reciting the "Affirmation for Receptivity":

"Lord, You are the Source and Fountain of all life, I humbly invoke Your Divine Blessing and Healing. I fully accept Your Divine Healing Energy, with gratitude and in full faith."
Repeat three times.

TOUCHING THE HEART CHAKRA

Crown-hand chakras technique is used for projecting Divine Energy. As a healer becomes more powerful, it is necessary for him to lightly touch his heart chakra with one hand to soften the projected Divine Energy. Otherwise, the patient may weaken or may even faint.

FOREHEAD-HAND CHAKRAS TECHNIQUE

For healers who are quite powerful and whose antahkarana or spiritual root ("crystal card" or "silver cord") is bigger than the head; it is better to use the forehead chakra as the source chakra for electric Violet Pranic Energy than the crown chakra. This technique is called forehead-hand-chakras technique. For very powerful healers, the use of the forehead chakra as the source chakra is milder, safer and more effective. The use of the crown chakra as the source chakra by very powerful healers is overwhelming to the patient's body and will produce a slower rate of healing. When using the forehead-hand chakras technique, it is still necessary to touch the heart chakra with one hand.

INVOCATION

Before healing, it is advisable for the healer to silently pray: "Lord, You are the Source and Fountain of all life; I humbly invoke Divine Guidance, Divine Healing and Divine Protection with gratitude and in full faith." The healer may also invoke the Divine Blessing of Archangels, great Prophets or Avatars, Saints, your Spiritual Teacher, Angels and Healing Ministers for help and healing. "Through my Spiritual Teacher, the Healing Angels and the Healing Ministers, I humbly invoke Divine Guidance, Divine Healing and Divine Protection, with gratitude and in full faith."

AFTER HEALING THE HEALER SHOULD SILENTLY GIVE THANKS

"Lord, thank you for Your Divine Blessing. To my Spiritual Teacher, the Healing Angels and Healing Masters, thank you for Your help and for the healing." The healer may use other prayers or improvise prayers for healing and thanksgiving.

Gratitude in Our Prayers and Thoughts

A sense of gratitude and indebtedness to others is an important wellspring of a generous and virtuous life. All people can recognize that they are indebted to their parents, who gave them birth and raised them at considerable sacrifice. Our indebtedness extends much further than that. Fundamentally, we are indebted to God our Creator and the powers of nature that nourish and sustain our lives. Then, since the food we eat travels from the soil to our dining table by passing through many hands—that cultivate, harvest, clean, package, transport, sell and prepare it—we should recognize that we rely on the labors of many people in order to survive. A sense of gratitude to others is thus acknowledging our interdependent existence; it is an antidote to the illusion of egoism. Such gratitude is recalled and expressed in the prayer of grace or thanks offered before meals.

Another dimension of gratitude is directed towards those who are responsible for our education and enlightenment in the way of truth and salvation. Gratitude towards one's teachers, and especially towards the sages and founders of religions who offered their lives to find the truth, is a proper attitude of faith. Most of all, we should be grateful to God, who quietly has been guiding and nurturing each person toward salvation, and without whose grace the world would be plunged in darkness.

Whatever you do, in word or deed, do everything in the name of the Lord Jesus, giving thanks to God the Father through him. Christianity. Colossians 3.17

O you who believe! Eat of the good things that we have provided for you, and be grateful to God, if it is Him that you worship. Islam. Qur'an 2.172; Colossians 3.17; Cf Psalm 100, p. 202

God created foods to be received with thanksgiving by those who believe and know the truth. For everything created by God is good, and nothing is to be rejected if it is received with thanksgiving; for then it is consecrated by the word of God and prayer. Christianity 1 Timothy 4,3-5

Abraham caused God's name to be mentioned by all the travelers whom he entertained. For after they had eaten and drunk, and when they arose to bless Abraham, he said to them, "Is it of mine that you have eaten? Surely it is of what belongs to God that you have eaten. So praise and bless Him by whose word the world was created." Judaism Talmud, Sota 10b

The unworthy man is ungrateful, forgetful of benefits (done to him). This ingratitude, this forgetfulness is congenial to mean people...But the worthy person is grateful and mindful of benefits done to him. This gratitude, this mindfulness, is congenial to the best people. Buddhism. Anguttara Niklaya i.61

One upon whom we bestow kindness but will not express gratitude, is worse than a robber who carries away our belongings. African Traditional Religions. Yoruba Proverb

Be not like those who honor their gods in prosperity and curse them in adversity. In pleasure or pain, give thanks! Judaism. Midrash, Mekilta to Exodus 20.20

Even if you cry your heart out, hurt your eyes by constant weeping and even if you lead the life of an ascetic till the end of the world, all these untiring efforts of yours will not be able to make compensation for a tithe of His good will and kindness, for His bounties and munificence and for His mercy and charity in directing you towards the path of truth and religion. Islam (Shiite). Nahjul Balagha, Khutba 57

It is God who has made the night for you, that you may rest therein, and the day, as that which helps you to see. Verily God is full of grace and bounty to men, yet most men give no thanks. It is God who has made for you the earth as a resting place, and the sky as a canopy, and has given you shape—and made your shapes beautiful—and has provided for you sustenance of things pure and good; such is God, your Lord. So glory to God, the Lord of the Worlds! Islam. Qur'an 40.61, 64

O my Father, Great Elder, I have no words to thank you, but with your deep wisdom, I am sure that you can see how I value your glorious gifts. O my Father, when I look upon your greatness, I am confounded with awe. O Great Elder, Ruler of all things earthly and heavenly, I am your warrior, Ready to act in accordance with your will. African Traditional Religions. Kikuya Prayer (Kenyan)

You, The World Honored One, are a great benefactor. By doing this rare thing, You taught and benefited us Out of your compassion towards us. No one will be able to repay your favors Even if he tries to do it For many hundreds of millions of kalpas, Bi ibe wukk be able to repay your favors Even if he bows to you respectfully, And offers you his hands or feet or anything else. No one will be able to repay your favors Even if he carries you on his head or shoulders And respects you from the bottom of his heart For as many kalpas As there are sands in the River Ganges. Buddhism. Lotus Sutra 4

Qur'an 40.61, 64: Cf. Qur'an 14.32-34, p.310; 16.10-18, p 141; 32.4-9, p. 126; Wadhans, M.5, p. 913. On gratitude to parents, see Qur'an 46.15-16, p. 249. Lotus Sutra 4: The value of the Buddha's teaching is immeasurable. It touches eternity, which all temporal phenomena rolled up together cannot hope to attain. Hence no temporal acts of gratitude can possibly be worthy of it. Cf. Myokonin, p. 774

All human bodies are things lent by God. With what thought are you using them? Terrikyo. Ofudesake 3.41

When a man is born, whoever he may be, there is born simultaneously a debt to the gods, to the sages, to the ancestors and to men. When he performs sacrifice it is the debt to the gods which is concerned. It is on their behalf, therefore, that he is taking action when he sacrifices or makes an oblation. And when he recites the Vedas that he is a guardian of the treasure store of the sages. And when he desires offspring, it is the debt to the ancestors which is concerned. It is on their behalf, therefore, that he is taking action, so that their offspring may continue, without interruption. And when he entertains guests, it is the debt to man which is concerned. It is on their behalf, therefore, that he is taking action if he entertains guests and gives them food and drink. The man who does all these things has performed a true work; he has obtained all, conquered all. Hinduism. Satapatha Brahmana 1.7.2.1-5

Ah, children—Be not arrogant, but Assist the deities of Marvelous spirit power In their work. Even the grains, and the Teeming grass and trees—Even these are favored with Blessings from Amaterasu, Great Goddess of the Sun. Morning and evening. At each meal you take, Consider the blessings of Toyouke-no-kami, You people of the world. The blessings of the Gods of heaven and earth—Without these, How could we exist, Even for a day, even for a night? Satapatha Brahmana 1.7.2.4: On gratitude to one's parents, cf. Anguttara Nikaya i.61, p 250; Classic on Filial Piety 1,p.249. Ofudesaki 3.41: Cf Sun Myung Moon, 9-30-79, p. 307.

Forget not the grace Of generations of ancestors; From age to age, the ancestors Are our own *ujigami*, Gods of our families. Father and mother Are gods of the family; Even so, honor them as gods with heartfelt service, All you of human birth. Shinto. Norinaga Motoori, One Hundred Poems on the Jewelled Spear.

One hundred Poems on the Jewelled Spear: The *ujigami* are eponymous ancestors of the clan; one's ancestors should be reverenced. Toyouke-no-kami is the Food Goddess worshipped at the Outer Shrine of the Temple at Ise, and Amaterasu is the Sun Goddess; they represent all the productive forces of nature and humanity which provide our food.

We feel gratitude for these many gifts, and strive to return for what we have been given by spreading gratitude wherever we live.

Genuine Gratitude Transformation of the Heart

By Mari Nagasawa

In the Broadway musical, Les Miserables, the transforming power of genuine gratitude is displayed by the man character, Jean Valjean.

The fugitive Valjean steals silver candlesticks from a priest who gave him shelter for the night. The police ambush the thief, but to Valjean's amazement, the priest says that he gave Valjean the candlesticks as a gift. Later, the priest rejects Valjean's attempt to return the candlesticks, and the criminal must wrestle with an uncomfortable feeling of gratitude. Gratitude gradually transforms the opportunist into a selfless, generous man.

Real, transforming gratitude like Valjean's is difficult to find. For instance, one would imagine that New York City Marathon runners, rather parched at the 20 mile mark, would experience genuine gratitude as they grab water from the hands of supporters. But the runners' gratitude is tainted with self-righteousness. The runners expect it; they feel they earn the water.

Even when a student receives a large Columbia University grant, his gratitude is minimal. He does not feel an increased school appreciation because deep down, he thinks he merits the aid, based on what he has achieved with his limited resources.

And when a New Yorker gives a tourist directions to the subway, the tourist does not realize that he might have had to ask ten people before getting a straight answer. He rationalizes that someone would have eventually helped him. So he is not very thankful to that particular person.

These three examples fail to illustrate real gratitude. The definition of gratitude is difficult to pin down. It occurs when one receives something needed and voluntarily given. If the gratitude is genuine, one will invariably want to please the giver in some way. The compulsion to return the favor is strong, not because one "has to," with a sense of obligation or guilt, but because one wants to bestow the same kind of joy upon the giver.

Unfortunately, the kind of thankfulness Valjean exhibited appears to have gone the way of the dinosaur.

Yet, it may be that the Christian understands gratitude. The Christian thinks he is a sinner, incapable of meeting God's standard of goodness (God's standard is Himself-perfection.) The believer's own hopeless state would send him into despair, if not for God's gift of life. Like Valjean, the believer is completely shocked at the demonstration of grace.

And if the priest's small sacrifice caused Valjean so much gratitude that he was transformed by it, then how much more grateful must Christians be for God's sacrifice of His only Son! Indeed, Christians claim that Jesus transforms their bodies of death into bodies of life.

> Just as Valjean grew to live selflessly, the gratitude of Christians irresistably compels them to do likewise. Ideally, coercion and personal gain have no place in their desire to do good in Christ's name. Otherwise, serving God becomes arduous and joyless. This is the nature of "dying to self" and "living to Christ" all that Christians do is loss, unless it is done to please their life-giver.

Then, it is not surprising that Christians often go to great lengths to serve God. Mother Theresa, one well-known example of a life of gratitude, traveled the world to bring the Gospel, aid and gradually the media's eye to dying communities, from small villages in India to New York City. Upon walking the streets of Manhattan, she said, "I've never seen so many lonely people."

"Also, full time missionaries give up financial and physical security for dangerous, backward countries in which to spread the Gospel. The sacrifices they make seem little to them, in comparison to that which Jesus made. Their gratitude enables them to take on otherwise daunting tasks.

In everyday life, Christians demonstrate their gratitude for Christ in little ways Christian students might give up studying time to pray for or counsel friends in need. Teachers might choose to explain all the ways in which evolution is not scientific. Faithful fathers put aside their own worldly hopes for their sons, and allow them to attend seminaries. Once touched by the enormity of Christ's death and resurrection, believers willingly die little deaths every day.

In the big picture, genuine gratitude increasingly permeates words and actions of believers, gradually shaping each person from inside out to be more and more like Christ. As believers mature, and are confronted with more and more of their sins and weaknesses, they find themselves increasingly grateful to God for His love.

The first stage of transformation is perhaps the most difficult, because it is the initial confrontation with the darkness in one's own soul. To accept God on His own terms means seeing one's own sinfulness, then trusting that through Christ's death and resurrection, God delivers one from the death that results from it.

But accepting Christ also entails a natural joyful thankfulness. This is a gratitude so powerful that one cannot help but share His love, which is an everlasting reservoir.

Gratitude Meditations

As you glance at the **G**, reflect on feeling Gratitude towards your friends, loved ones, and others to whom you feel gratitude. Breathe in and out at a slow regular rate and fixate on the warm feelings of thanks and appreciation that come to you as you recall what others have done for you and what you have been able to do for them. Give thanks to yourself for all the good deeds you have done. Give thanks to them for all they have done for you. Get into the attitude of gratitude where you feel inner peace, in relationship to the objects of your gratitude. Little things don't bother you. Just feel Good. As you feel thankful, imagine how you can enlarge and expand your feelings of gratitude to encompass all in your life, the people you contact every day and spread a little sunshine where you go into the lives of those you contact today. Thank you for visiting. I wish you love and gratitude. Just look at G and meditate and wonder what it would be like if we all lived a life of gratitude.

G

These feelings of gratitude will stimulate your generosity and you will spring forth into action and spread gratitude around the world in which you live.

Our Gratitude mantra is: Geeeeeeeeeeeeeeeeeeeeeeeeee, repeated about once every 5-10 seconds, silently or out loud depending on where we are and what we feel like. As you silently say Geeeeeeeeeeeeeeeeeeeeeeeeee, remember the gifts you have been given by your parents, teachers, family, friends and colleagues. Feel gratitude for the hurts, and the pains, and the rejections and all the things you got that you did not want, in addition to the wondrous gifts you wanted and were given.

Living Gratitude

It's so easy to take life for granted. Every morning when we awaken there's another whole day lying before us, just like there was yesterday, and the day before. Most of those days we probably didn't have to worry too much about life's basics—food, clothing, roof, family, friends. Day following upon day, season upon season, can become routine. Nothing much to get excited about. But the longer I've lived, the more grateful I've become for each day, and for all it brings. What a gift, a privilege, a joy it is to be alive today. What a wonder it is to breathe the earth's air, to feel the warm sun or the cold rain, to float through the moments of each day.

Life, and all it contains, is totally gratuitous, a 100% gift. I didn't bring myself into existence, nor is it I who keep myself going. I'm merely the recipient of this awesome gift. I didn't create the molecules of air I breathe in, nor the photons of light that strike my eye. I did not create the language I use to think with and to chat with you. It's all a gift. Each moment, every beat of my heart, each electronic impulse within my brain, every mouthful of food I eat, and thread of clothing I wear, each person that cares for me, and those that don't, they are all a blessing, the work of a Hand infinitely greater than my own.

Countless creatures and generations have come before us. But right now it's our turn to walk the beautiful earth, to drink its refreshing waters, to work through its challenges, to be born and give birth, to love and be loved, to grow and share, to suffer and die. One moment in earth's history is brief, a mere spark in the night, and it's no good trying to hold on to it. It's for us to enjoy and celebrate, to relish each day and cherish each person, but to hold all things gently, ever ready to let go.

The only reasonable response to the gift of life is gratitude—gratitude to the Creator as a constant disposition of heart. Gratefulness of heart is a humble acknowledgement of our indebtedness, our creatureliness. It is expressed more in making good use of our gifts, and sharing them, than in words. Living in gratitude we are always praying, praising and thanking our bountiful God for the wondrous gift of life.

In the evening, when I lie in bed and end my prayers with the words, "I thank you, God, for all that is good and clear and beautiful," I am filled with joy...I don't think then of all the misery, but of the beauty that still remains...My advice is "Go outside, to the fields, enjoy nature and the sunshine, go out and try to recapture happiness in yourself and in God. Think of all the beauty that's still left in and around you and be happy!"...I've found that there is always some beauty left—in nature, sunshine, freedom, in yourself: these can all help you. Look at these things, then you find yourself again, and God, and then you regain your balance.

Anne Frank: The Diary of a Young Girl Tuesday, 7 March, 1944

Looking for Gratitude Opportunities

Gratitude is a state of mind that is built up with regular consistent work and application. You need to be aware of it much of your waking time and see the world through the eyes of gratitude. When patients start out doing this, they call it a "stretch". It might be called putting a gratitude "spin" on events in the world. However, if that leads to a desired outcome state for you, your family and society, that is a great idea.

You need to develop the habit of looking forward to gratitude opportunities. These are life situations that you may recall and write down in your Gratitude Journal at night before you go to sleep. This Attitude of Gratitude is looking to appreciate things small, medium and large. You look for the beauty of the day and the color of the leaves and feel gratitude for beauty. You look for the wonders of rain and snow and the opportunity they present of helping others. You feel gratitude for breakfast, lunch and dinner, and always to Your Country in which all this is happening for you and yours. You have enthusiasm and excitement as you work with others to correct their negative states of mind and the results of envy and jealousy. America is beautiful.

"You can spread gratitude around" one of my patients mentioned to me as she described a conversation her 10 year old daughter had with a 10 year old friend, while driving in the car. The friend said, " I don't have as many friends as Julie. Everyone likes her more than me." Then she said, "Julie has a bigger house than me and nicer clothes." At that point, the daughter intervened and told her friend that she should feel happy for the house that she lives in, which with its five bedrooms was "big enough." The daughter said that she was the girl's friend and liked her a lot, as much or more than she liked Julie, and that she should feel grateful for that. The 10 year old thought awhile a said, "I guess you are right. I am happy I have a nice house and a nice mother; Julie's mother isn't so nice. I should be happy with what I have." The daughter was repeating words she had heard from my patient who was delighted and said that "It spreads around."

A gratitude opportunity is the chance to spread gratitude around and when enough is spread around, it might change the consciousness of the world. We will always struggle with envy, jealousy, greed and the negative thinking that comes from these problems, because the brain is composed of difference detector neurons and creates differences by the way it works, but if you are armed with the attitude of gratitude, then it is easier not to get carried away with these base feelings. Gratitude is the leaven that softens the perception of differences that leads to so much human splendor and misery.

I counsel my patients to feel grateful when they are hungry, when they do not get the food they want to eat, and when they feel empty. At first they look at me with scorn, for that is an odd way for them to think. But when they "get it", they realize that accepting their hunger and feeling of emptiness, instead of acting out and eating until they are full, is the logical way to act because they want to lose weight, feel slender and good about themselves. What starts as an "Oh, yeah", quizzical note of scorn, turns into a smile and a feeling that the idea isn't so crazy after all. Hunger and feeling the discomfort of wanting to eat and not eating, is a gratitude opportunity. You have to put back in for what you have been given to show your gratitude. You were given a nice body and a pretty face when you were a child, and it is your obligation to take care of them, by eating properly and working out and meditating and living a balanced life.

You can look for gratitude in the opportunity to do a favor for a friend and feel grateful for the opportunity.

Gratitude can overcome your shyness, when you realize that if you are being grateful when you display your talents and enjoy the experience of coming out of the shyness box because you feel grateful for what you have been given and feel grateful for the opportunity to display what you have achieved with what you were given through your hard work.

The motive of your conduct changes when you are looking for gratitude. You act in order to put something back in for what you have been given. This fulfilling of obligation gives you power and makes you strong and you feel good about your strengths. When your strengths are liberated, you do not have to live trapped inside of the box of your shyness and your weakness. Give your all to America.

Things to Feel Grateful For From Unity of Phoenix
www.unityphx.org

This year's 40 days are over, but you can use these lessons any time!
Sunday, October 15—I am Grateful
Monday, October 16—I am Grateful for an Open Mind
Tuesday, October 17—I am Grateful for God's Infinite Good
Wednesday, October 18—I am Grateful for All My Blessings
Thursday, October 19—I am Grateful for the City in Which I Live
Friday, October 20—I am Grateful for My Ability to Say No
Saturday, October 21—I am Grateful for All the Time to do what is Mine to do
Sunday, October 22—I am Grateful for an Open Door
Monday, October 23—I am Grateful for Honesty
Tuesday, October 24—I am Grateful for Honor
Wednesday, October 25—I am Grateful for Silent Stillness
Thursday, October 26—I am Grateful for the Ability to Ask
Friday, October 27—I am Grateful for My Gift of Perseverance
Saturday, October 28—I am Grateful that I Don't Know
Sunday, October 29—I am Grateful for Beauty
Monday, October 30—I am Grateful for My Ability to Forgive
Tuesday, October 31—I am Grateful for Unseen Good
Wednesday, November 1—I am Grateful for This New Month
Thursday, November 2—I am Grateful for My Integrity
Friday, November 3—I am Grateful for Courage
Saturday, November 4—I am Grateful for My Ability to Find a Blessing
Sunday, November 5—I am Grateful for My Power of Determination
Monday, November 6—I am Grateful that I use My Time Constructively
Tuesday, November 7—I am Grateful for My Facility of Judgement
Wednesday, November 8—I am Grateful I Dream with an Innocent Spirit
Thursday, November 9—I am Grateful for an Unknown Future
Friday, November 10—I am Grateful for My Ability to "Go for it"
Saturday, November 11—I am Grateful for Everyone Who has Gone Before Me.
Sunday, November 12—I am Grateful for my Body
Monday, November 13—I am Grateful for Circulation
Tuesday, November 14—I am Grateful for my Sense of Appreciation and I Show it Today
Wednesday, November 15—I am Grateful for the Child Within
Thursday, November 16—I am Grateful for a Forgiving Heart
Friday, November 17—I am Grateful that I am a Blessing

Saturday, November 18—I am Grateful for My Wonderful Mind
Sunday, November 19—I am Grateful for completions
Monday, November 20—I am Grateful for My Spiritual Vision
Tuesday, November 21—I am Grateful for my Ability to Compliment
Wednesday, November 22—I am Grateful for Life
Thursday, November 23—I am Grateful for the World and Everything and
    Everyone in it

On Gratitude from the Internet Excite Search Engine

URL: http//boris.qub.qc.uk/archives/fox/fox-11-1996/0129.html
Summary: edu) Dte: Wed, 13 Nov 1996 20:54:00—0600 (CST) As we approach
the Thanksgiving season and Advent, I am captivated by the idea of gratitude. Is
life a bitch, and then you die, or is life a feast, a rare jewel that bristles with a
radiance too magnificent to grasp...and what in the Universe determines who
experiences what?

URL: http://www.indirect.com/www/beauty/beauty gram11.htm
Summary: Past offenses of some leaders in the churches have turned off many
people and with it their daily routine of gratitude before meals. It seems that
every once in a while we truly glimpse other people's difficulties and then begin
for a temporary moment to count our blessings and be grateful for what we have.
60% James E. Talmage on Gratitude

URL: http//www.xmission.com/-dkenison/lds/gtp/arc/jet_grat.html
Summary: Our old friend, Izaak Walton—he of fishing rod and stream—
expressed this amusing thought: "God has two dwellings: one in heaven, and the
other in a meek and thankful heart." The man who has come into close
communion with God cannot fail to be thankful; for he feels, he knows, that for
all he has and all he is, he is indebted to the Supreme Giver, and one would think
that there is no.

URL: http://www.sonic.net/~robd/alanon/messages/293.html
Summary: [Follow Ups] [Post Followup] [Friends of Alanon] [FAQ] Posted by
Barbs on July 19, 1997 at 15:22:30: Today I can work on my attitude. I can start
it in the morning by doing something good for myself—a walk, even though it
may follow the same path daily, there are many things along the way that
constantly change (as I do when working my program) clouds, flowers, people,
etc.
60% Gratitude Grows Into Happiness by Annie Y. Zaleszsak

Monte J. Meldman M.D.

URL: http://www/cadvision com/intouch/annie.html
Summary: Products and Services * Angels* Random Acts of Kindness*
Submission Call.
Products and Services * Angels * Random Acts of Kindness * Submission Call
60% Gratitude Grows Into Happiness by Annie Y. Zaleszsak

URL: http://www.intouchmag.com/annie.html
Summary: To whom or what the gratitude is expressed does not seem to matter;
the key is expression. The act of expressing gratitude perpetuates a sense of love
of all things created.

URL: http://www.familyville.com/data/bible/People/issue012.html
Summary: When I see a handicapped person, I am prompted to realize that I
could be without my senses, or limbs, mobility, etc, when I should be thanking
God every day. Just as people have thresholds of physical pain, we have
thresholds of emotional pain.

Spreading Gratitude

How can I spread my gratitude? First by saying, "Thank You". Next, by writing it down in my Gratitude Journal. Then by putting something back in for what I have been given. You give a gift in exchange for the gift you have been given. Turns out, this is a lot like negative revenge. Instead of returning a hurt for a hurt, you exchange a gift for a gift. You "put something back in" for what you have been given.

Ted Turner put one billion dollars back into the United Nations. Reggie White, the defensive tackle of the Green Bay Packers, puts himself back into the community and works to help less fortunate children to improve their lot in life. Each of us in our own way can return for the gift we have been given, and spread our gratitude around our world.

In the spiritual realm, we can follow the commandments and live a good life performing the obligations that we have been given by God. In the Christian realm, we can accept the gift of Christ and pay God back for that supreme sacrifice and example of love. We can always do unto others as they have done unto us and when we are living in the state of gratitude we can return love for love instead of hurt for hurt. This leads to a wonderful feeling of wholeness and completion. It is wonderful to let go of hate and hold on to gratitude. This lets the positive forces of your life spring onto the forefront as you engage in a social interest in order to pay back for the gift of your life. You always know what to do next when you are living on gratitude. You accept the gift that is given to you and pay back for what you have been given..

Living your life in gratitude keeps you away from violence and robbing and stealing and vandalism. Gratitude is the opposite of murder and is a life creating force that can be shared in the community. You can publish your gratitude in the newspapers and on the Internet and then spend your life living up to your own words as they have been written and published.

Give thanks by doing good works. Gratitude in action is the highest form of gratitude.

Gratitude Books

Andy and the Lion: A Tale of Kindness Remembered or the Power of Gratitude (Picture Puffins) James Henry Daugherty / Paperback / Pub. Price: $4.99 Barnes and Noble Price: $3.99

The Book of Giving: Poems of Thanks, Praise & Celebration by Kay Chorao/Hardcover; Pub. Price: $16.99. B&N Price: $11.89—

Count Your Blessings! John F. Demartini / Paperback / Pub. Price $14.95 B&N Price: $11.96—

Envy & Gratitude & Other Works, 1946-1963, Vol. 3 Melanie Klein/Hardcover B&N Price $53.75

Grace & Gratitude: The Eucharistic Theology of John Calvin B. A. Gerrish/ Paperback/ Pub. Price: $13.95 B&N Price $11.16

Gratefulness, the Heart of Prayer: An Approach to Life in Fullness-David Steindl-Rast/ Paperback / Pub. Price: $11.95 B&N Price $9.56

Gratitude: Terrance C. McConnell / Hardcover / Pub. Price $39.95 B&N Price $27.96—

Gratitude: Louise L. Hay, Jill Kramer (Editor) / Paperback / Pub. Price: $12.95. B&N price: $10.36

Gratitude in a Jar Honor/ Paperback / Pub. Price $10.00 B&N price: $8.00—

The Gratitude of Kings: Marion Zimmer Bradley / Hardcover/ Pub. Price: $13.95 B&N Price: $9.76

Gratitude: Reflections on What We Owe to our Country by William F. Buckley, Jr. Audio: B&N price: $22.95

I Can't Make a Flower: North. American Ed. Margaret Spivey, Diana Catchpole (Illustrator)/ Paperback/Pub Price: $8.00 B&N Price: $6.40

Learning to Dream Again: From Grief to Gratitude: Charles B. Bugg/Paperback. Pub Price: $7.95 B&N Price $6.36

Many Thanks: Loving Thoughts for All Occasions: Lisa Palas Hardcover Pub Price: $7.99 B&N price: $5.59

New Life in God's World: Doris Willis, pat Karch (Illustrator) Paperback / Pub Price: $3.95 B&N Price: $3.16

The Next Step: A Guide for Balanced Recovery: Todd Weber / Paperback. Pub. Price $8.95 B&N Price: $7.16

Next Step Workbook: Exercises in Gratitude, Forgiveness & Balance: Todd Weber / Paperback $7.95

Old Winter: Judith Benet Richardson; R.W. Alley (Illustrator Hardcover B&N Price $15.99

The Power of appreciation: A New Approach to Personal & Relational Healing by Adrian van Kaan, Susan Annette Muto / Paperback / Pub Price $10.95 B&N Price $8.76

Rebecca: A Father's Journey from Grief to Gratitude by Robert Jonas/Hardcover Pub Price $16.95

Recognition, Gratitude & Celebration by Patrick Townsend, Joan Gebhardt / Paperback Pub Price $12.95

Simple Abundance Journal of Gratitude: Living by Your Own Lights by Sarah Ban Breathnach / Hardcover / Pub Price $12.95

Sufism V: Gratitude, Patience, Trust in God, Aspiration, Veracity, Zeal, Valor, Althuism, Shame, Vol. 5 Javad Nurbakhsh, Terry Graham(Translator) Paperback

Thank You by Liesl Vazquez/ Hardcover/Pub Price $6.95

About The Author

Monte J. Meldman M.D. is a board certified psychiatrist who has specialized in the treatment of people with addictions. He has treated thousands of alcoholics, drug addicts, and obese people in many different settings—in hospital programs, in the office, in individual therapy and in groups. Gratitude is a central theme in recovering from addictions and Dr. Meldman explores gratitude as a healing tool in detail in this book. Gratitude is both a feeling and a doing, a becoming obligated and paying back for what you have been given. Gratitude healing is intended to help people transition from the ingrate state into the attitude of gratitude that is typical of a recovering person. If you work on the book and with Doctor you will install a gratitude button on your person that you can use whenever you need to transition from the ingrate state to the mood of gratitude. Dr. Meldman trained in psychiatry at Cincinnati General Hospital. He has written four other books and over one hundred articles published in peer reviewed articles. He feels gratitude much of the time and when he slips into the ingrate state he works on Gratitude Healing to restore his attitude of gratitude and bring that to others in his practice and life.